KU-197-085

Spurgeon's Sermons
on
Old Testament
Men

Book Two

C. H. Spurgeon Resources

Commenting and Commentaries
Day by Day with C. H. Spurgeon (compiled by Al Bryant)
The Treasury of David (edited by David Otis Fuller)
Spurgeon's Sermon Illustrations
Spurgeon's Sermon Notes
Spurgeon's Sermons on Angels
Spurgeon's Sermons on Christmas and Easter
Spurgeon's Sermons on the Cross of Christ
Spurgeon's Sermons on Family and Home
Spurgeon's Sermons on New Testament Men • Book One
Spurgeon's Sermons on New Testament Miracles
Spurgeon's Sermons on New Testament Women • Book One
Spurgeon's Sermons on Old Testament Men • Book One
Spurgeon's Sermons on Old Testament Men • Book Two
Spurgeon's Sermons on Old Testament Women • Book One
Spurgeon's Sermons on Old Testament Women • Book Two
Spurgeon's Sermons on the Parables of Christ
Spurgeon's Sermons on Great Prayers of the Bible
Spurgeon's Sermons on the Resurrection of Christ
Spurgeon's Sermons on Soulwinning
Spurgeon's Sermons on Special Days and Occasions

Spurgeon's Sermons on
Old Testament Men

Book Two

CHARLES HADDON SPURGEON

kregel
PUBLICATIONS

Grand Rapids, MI 49501

Spurgeon's Sermons on Old Testament Men • *Book Two*
by Charles H. Spurgeon

Copyright © 1995 by Kregel Publications.

Published by Kregel Publications, a division of Kregel, Inc., P.O. Box 2607, Grand Rapids, MI 49501. Kregel Publications provides trusted, biblical publications for Christian growth and service. Your comments and suggestions are valued.

All rights reserved. No part of this book may be reproduced, stored in a retrieval system, or transmitted in any form or by any means—electronic, mechanical, photocopy, recording, or otherwise—without written permission of the publisher, except for brief quotations in printed reviews.

Cover artwork: Don Ellens
Cover and book design: Alan G. Hartman

Library of Congress Cataloging-in-Publication Data

Spurgeon, C. H. (Charles Haddon), 1834–1892.
   [Sermons on Old Testament men]
   Spurgeon's Sermons on Old Testament men, book two / by Charles H. Spurgeon.
     p.   cm.
   1. Bible. O.T. Biography—Sermons. 2. Sermons, English. I. Title. II. Title: Sermons on Old Testament men. III. Series: Spurgeon, C. H. (Charles Haddon), 1834–1892. C. H. Spurgeon sermon series.
BS571.5.S68   1995   221.9'22—dc20   94-13313
                                     CIP

ISBN 0-8254-3789-x (pbk.)

1 2 3 4 5 printing / year 99 98 97 96 95

Printed in the United States of America

Contents

1

Adam: God's First Words to the First Sinner

The Lord God called unto Adam, and said unto him, Where art thou? (Genesis 3:9).

It will be interesting to the members of this church to know that it was under a sermon delivered by Mr. William Wallin from this very text that my honored and venerable predecessor, Dr. Gill, was converted to a knowledge of the truth as it is in Jesus. I looked with some degree of curiosity to his interpretation of this passage. I had half hoped to find there some allusion to his own conversion, but I did not, although I was edified by his clear and methodical comment upon it, to which I am under obligations for suggesting the present discourse. May I hope that, as this text has been the means in the hand of God of conferring upon the church of Christ a man who valiantly defended the truth of God and was the means of expounding the doctrine of grace with great clearness, that there may be here present today someone at least who, like John Gill, may hear the Word with power and may receive it in its quickening influence into his soul. No, let us pray that not one alone but that many may hear the inquiry of God as it rings through the multitude, and while it reaches the ear may it reach the heart too, and may some be brought before God in answer to the question "Where art thou?" and receive the assurance of pardon and go on their way in peace.

It is not necessary that I should, in expounding this text, enter at all into the circumstances which led to the inquiry. Man had sinned against God. Mark the *alienation of heart* which sin causes in the sinner. Adam ought to have sought out his Maker. He should have gone through the

---

This sermon was taken from *The Metropolitan Tabernacle Pulpit* and was preached on Sunday morning, October 6, 1861.

garden crying for his God, "My God, my God, I have sinned against You. Where are *You?* Low at Your feet Your creature falls and asks mercy at Your hands. My Father, You have placed me in this lovely Paradise; I have wickedly and willfully eaten of the fruit of which You said that I should not eat of it, since in the day late thereof I should surely die. Behold, my Father, I submit to the penalty. I confess Your justice and beseech Your mercy, if mercy can be shown to such an one as I am." But instead thereof, Adam flies from God. The sinner comes not to God; God comes to him. It is not "My God, where art thou?" but the first cry is the voice of grace, "Sinner, where art *thou?*" God comes to man; man seeks not his God. Despite all the doctrines which proud free-will has manufactured, there has never been found from Adam's day until now a single instance in which the sinner first sought his God. God must first seek him. The sheep strays of itself, but it never returns to its fold unless sought by the Great Shepherd. It is human to err; it is divine to repent. Man *can* commit iniquity, but even to know that it is iniquity so as to feel the guilt of it is the gift of the grace of God. We have and are nothing but what is vile. Everything which is Godlike, everything which aspires toward righteousness and true holiness comes from the Most High.

And while the text manifestly teaches us the alienation of the human heart from God so that man shuns his Maker and does not desire fellowship with Him, it reveals also *the folly* which sin has caused. Sin made man a fool. He was once in God's image, wise; now, since the trail of the serpent has passed over his nature, he has become an arrant fool, for is not he a fool who would cover the nakedness of sin with fig leaves? Is not he indeed mad who would hide from the omniscient Jehovah beneath the spreading of boughs of trees? Did not Adam know that God fills all space and dwells everywhere, that from the highest heaven to the deepest hell there is nothing that is hid from His understanding? and yet so ignorant and stupid is he that he hopes to escape from God and make the trees of the garden a covert from the fiery eyes of divine wrath. Ah! how foolish we are! How we repeat the folly of our first parent every day when we seek to hide sin from conscience and then think it is hidden from God; when we are more afraid of the gaze of man than of the searchings of the Eternal One; when because the sin is secret and has not entrenched upon the laws and customs of society, we make no conscience of it but go to our beds with the black mark still upon us, being satisfied because man does not see it, that therefore God does not perceive it. O sin, you have made man ask the question, "Whither shall I flee from thy presence?" and you have made him forget that if he ascend to heaven, God is there; if he make his bed in hell, God is there, and if he says, "Surely the darkness shall cover me," even the night shall be light about him.

But now, the Lord Himself comes forth to Adam, and note how He comes. He comes *walking*. He was in no haste to smite the offender, not flying upon wings of wind, not hurrying with His fiery sword unsheathed, but *walking* in the garden. *"In the cool of the day"*—not in the dead of night, when the natural glooms of darkness might have increased the terrors of the criminal; not in the heat of the day, lest he should imagine that God came in the heat of passion; not in the early morning, as if in haste to slay, but at the close of the day, for God is longsuffering, slow to anger, and of great mercy; but in the cool of the evening, when the sun was setting upon Eden's last day of glory, when the dews began to weep for man's misery, when the gentle winds with breath of mercy breathed upon the hot cheek of fear; when earth was silent that man might meditate, and when heaven was lighting her evening lamps, that man might have hope in darkness; then, and not until then, forth came the offended Father. Adam flies and seeks to avoid that very God whom he had once met with confidence and with whom he had the sweetest fellowship, talking with Him as a man talks with his friend.

And now hear the voice of God as He cries, "Adam, where art thou?" Oh! there were two truths in that short sentence. It showed that *Adam was lost*, or God would not have needed to ask him where he was. Until we have lost a thing, we need not inquire about it; but when God said, "Adam, where art thou?" it was the voice of a shepherd inquiring for his lost sheep; or better still, the cry of a loving parent asking for his child that has ran away from him, "Where art thou?" There are but three words, but they contain the dread doctrine of our lost estate. When *God* asks, "Where art thou?" man must be lost. When God Himself inquires where he is, he must be lost in a more awful sense than you and I have as yet fully known. But then, there was also mercy here, for it showed that God intended to have mercy upon man, or else He would have let him remain lost and would not have said, "Where art thou?"

Men do not inquire for what they do not value. There was a Gospel sermon, I think, in those three divine words as they penetrated the dense parts of the thicket and reached the tingling ears of the fugitives—"Where art thou?" Your God is not willing to lose you; He is come forth to seek you, just as by-and-by He means to come forth in the person of His Son, not only to seek but to save that which now is lost. "Where art thou, Adam?" Oh, had God meant to have destroyed the race, He would have hurled His thunderbolt at once and burned the trees and let the ashes of the sinner lie beneath His angry gaze. He would have rushed in the whirlwind and in the storm, and tearing up the cedars and the pomegranates by their roots, He would have said, "Here you are, you rebel; traitor, take your due deserts! let hell open before you, and be you swallowed up forever." But no, He loves man; He cares for him and therefore now inquires where he is in tones of calmness, "Adam, where art thou, where art thou?"

The question which the Lord asked of Adam may be used in five different ways. We are not sure in what precise sense the Lord intended it—perhaps in all—for there is always in the utterance of the Divine One a great depth which couches beneath. Our words, if they give one sense, do well; but the Lord knows how to speak so that He shall teach many truths in few words. We give little in much; God gives much in little. Many words and little sense—this is too often the rule of man's speech. Few words and much meaning—this is the rule with God. We give gold beaten out into leaf; God gives ingots of gold when He speaks. We use but the fillings of gems; God drops pearls from His lips each time He speaks to us, nor shall we, perhaps, even in eternity, know how divine are God's words—how like Himself, how exceeding broad, how infinite.

The Inquiry of God Was Intended in an Arousing Sense

Sin stultifies the conscience, it drugs the mind, so that after sin man is not so capable of understanding his danger as he would have been without it. Sin is a poison which kills conscience painlessly by mortification. Men sleep and sleep and sleep and sleep on until death closes the scene, and then in hell they awake in torments. One of the first works of grace in a man is to put aside this sleep, to startle him from his lethargy, to make him open his eyes and discover his danger. One of the first deeds of the Good Physician is to put sensibility into our flesh. It has become cold and dead and mortified; he puts life into it, and then there is pain; but that very pain has a salutary effect upon us. Now, I think that this question from the Lord was intended to set Adam thinking. "Where art thou?" He had perceived in some degree into what a state his sin had brought him, but this question was meant to stir the depths of his spirit and wake him up to such a sense of danger that he should labor to escape from the wrath to come. "Adam, where art thou?"—look at yourself now, naked, a stranger to your God, dreading the presence of your Maker, miserable, undone. "Adam, where art thou?"—with a hard heart, with a rebellious will, fallen, fallen, fallen from your high estate. "Adam, where art thou?" Lost, lost to your God, lost to happiness, lost to peace, lost in time, lost in eternity. *Sinner, "where art thou?"* O that I might, by the earnest words which I shall now utter, stir up some callous, careless sinner to answer the inquiry for himself! Man, where are you?—where are you this morning? Shall I tell you? You are in a condition in which your very conscience condemns you. How many there are of you who have never repented of sin, have never believed in Christ! I ask you, is your conscience easy?—is it always easy? Are there not some times when the thunderer will be heard? Are there not seasons when the watchman lights his candle and searches the secret parts of your soul and discovers your iniquity? Where are you, then?—for conscience is to God what the hook is to the fisherman. Conscience, like God's hook, is in your jaws today, and He has but to draw in the line, and you are in the consuming fire. Though conscience makes you smart, justice shall be far sterner with you than your poor imperfect conscience. If your heart condemns you, God is greater than your heart and knows all things. Your conscience tells you you are wrong—O how wrong, then, must you be!

But man, do you not know you are a stranger from your God? Many of you seldom think of Him. You can spend days and weeks without a mention of His name, except, perhaps, in some trivial language or in an oath. You cannot live without a friend, but you can live without your God. You eat, you drink, you are satisfied; the world is enough for you; its transient pleasures satisfy your spirit. If you saw God here, you would flee from Him; you are an enemy to Him. Oh! is this the right case for a creature to be in? Let the question come to you—"Where art thou?" Must not that creature be in a very pitiable position who is afraid of his Creator? You were made to glorify Him; you were made to rejoice in His presence and to delight in His goodness; but it seems you love not the very food which was meant to sustain you. You must be sick—you must be sick indeed! "Where art thou?" Remember, the Almighty God is angry with you. His commandments, like so many guns charged to the muzzle, are all pointed against you this morning; and it needs only the uplifted finger of the Divine one, and they shall soon destroy you and break you in pieces. Would a man be comfortable with his neck upon the block and the ax gleaming above his head? It is your case today. You are in the position of the courtier at the feast of Dionysius with the sword over your head suspended by a single hair. Condemned already!! "God is angry with the wicked every day." "If he turn not, he will whet his sword: he hath bent his bow and made it ready." Where are you, man? O God, help the man to see where he is! Open his eyes; let the question startle him. Let him start in his sleep a little—aye, let him wake and discover where he is—obnoxious to Your wrath and the object of Your hot displeasure!

"Where art thou?" Your life is frail; nothing can be more weak. A spider's line is a cable compared with the thread of your life. Dreams are substantial masonry compared with the bubble structure of your being. You are here and you are gone. You sit here today; before another week is past you may be howling in another world. Oh, where are you man? Unpardoned, and yet a dying man! Condemned, yet going carelessly toward destruction! Covered with sin, yet speeding to your Judge's dread tribunal! Lost here, yet hurrying on, each moment bearing you on eagle's wings to the place where you shall be lost eternally! How hard it is to bring ourselves to know ourselves! In other matters if a man be a little sick, he seeks his doctor and would know his position; but here a man says, "Peace, peace: let well alone." If we fear that our personal estates are at all in jeopardy, we have anxious nights and toilsome days; but, oh! our souls—our poor, poor souls—we play with them as if they were worthless counters or bits of platter which a child might pick up in the streets and cast away! Sinner! sinner! sinner! is your soul so poor a bauble that you can afford to lose it because you will not break your sleep and stay your pleasurable dreams! Oh, if a brother's heart can move your heart, and if a brother's voice can wake your sleeping eyes, I would say, "What ails you, O sleeper? Arise, and call upon your God! Awake! why do you sleep! Awake to answer the question, 'Where art thou?'—lost, ruined, and undone! O sinner where are you?"

The Question Was Meant to Convince of Sin and Lead to a Confession

Had Adam's heart been in a right state, he would have made a full confession of his sinfulness. "Where art thou?" Let us hear the voice of God saying that to us, if today we are out of God and out of Christ. "Where are you, Adam? I made you in Mine own image; I made you a little lower than the angels; I made you to have dominion over the works of My hands; I put all things under you feet—the fowl of the air and the fish of the sea and whatsoever passes through the depths of the sea. I gave this whole garden of delights to be your home. I honored you with My presence; I thought of your welfare and forestalled all your desires. The moon did not hurt you by night; the sun did not smite you by day. I tempered the winds for you; I clothed the trees with fruit for your nourishment. I made all things minister to your happiness. Where are you? I asked of you but that little thing that you would not touch one tree which I had reserved for Myself. Where are you? Are you in the room of a thief, a rebel, a traitor? Have you sinned? O Adam, where are you?"

And now, sinner, hear me. "Where art thou?" To many of you the Lord might say, "I gave you a godly mother who wept over you in your childhood. I gave you a holy father who longed for your conversion. I gave you the gifts of Providence—you never wanted for a meal. I clothed your back. I put you in a comfortable position in life. I raised you up from a bed of sickness. I overlooked ten thousand follies. My mercies like a river have flown to you. When I opened your eyes in the morning, it was to look upon My goodness; and until the last moment of the night I was your helper and drew the curtains about your defenseless head. I have covered you with My feathers; under my wings have you trusted, and now *where are you?* Have you not forgotten My commandments, abhorred My person, broken My laws, rejected My Son? Are You not at this day a disbeliever, content to trust to your own works but not to take the finished righteousness of my beloved Son, the Savior of the world? What have you done for Him who has done so much for you? What are you? Have you not been a cumber-ground—a tree that sucks the soil but bears no fruit—that drinks in the genial rain of heaven but yields no grateful fruit? Where are you? Are you not today in the camp of My enemy? Are you not on Satan's side, defying Me, and lifting up the puny arm of your rebellion against the Lord that made you and that keeps the breath in your nostrils—in whose hand your life is, and whose are all your ways? Sinner, where are you? After all God's goodness—still a sinner!"

Read the question again thus, "Where art thou?" The serpent said you should be a god. You thought to be made exceeding glorious. Is it so, Adam? Is it so? Where is your boasted knowledge? Where the honors? Where the vast attainments that rebellion would bring to you? Instead of the clothing of angels, you are naked; instead of glory, you have shame; instead of preferment, you have disgrace. Adam, where are you? And sinner, where are *you?* Sin said to you, I will give you pleasure—you have had it; but what of the pain which followed the pleasure. Sin gave you its cup full of mixed wine; but what of the red eyes and of the woe? Sin said to you, "I will make you great"; but what has it done for you? Drunkard, what has it done for you? Given you rags and poverty. Adulterer, fornicator, what has it done for you? Filled your flesh with leprosy and your soul with agony. Thief! cheat! what has it done for you? Disgraced you and branded you before the eyes of men. Sinner in secret! polite sinner! what has it done for you? Soured your sweets, and poisoned all your joys. Where are you—where are you? In every case sin has been a liar; and without exception, rebellion, if it has not yet brought its due deserts, will do so, and sinners shall be filled with their own ways.

And then to add to the conviction, the Lord asks of Adam, "Where art thou?" as if He asked him, "How did you come there?" Adam, you came there of yourself. If you had been upright, Eve had not cast you down. Eve, 'twas not the serpent with whom the main guilt must lie; had you not given ear, he might have tempted long if you had been deaf. And so today God says to the sinner, "Where art thou?" You are where you have brought yourself. That you have sinned is your own fault and none else's but your own. Oh, it is hard to make a sinner see

that sin is his own property. It is the only thing we have. There is only
one thing we created, and that is sin, and that is our own. If I permit
anything that is evil, I must confess it is a child that has sprung from
my own bowels; it has its origin in myself. If we talk of the fall, men
will throw their sin on father Adam. They speak of the depravity of nature, and then they think they are to be excused; as if depravity of nature did not prove the man to be desperately bad, as if it were not
saying that sin is essentially man's own thing, that he has it in his very
bones and in his blood. If we be sinners, there is no excuse for us whatever, and if we live and die so, the guilt shall lie at our own door, but
nowhere else. "Adam, where art thou?" Thou art where you have willfully put yourself, and you remain willfully in the same desperate state
of rebellion against God and of alienation from Him.

I would God that something would not only arouse the sinner this
morning but work conviction in him. It is easier to make a man start in
his sleep than to make him rise and burn the loathsome bed on which
he slumbered, and this is what the sinner must do and what he will do if
God be at work with him. He will wake up to find himself lost; conviction will give him the consciousness that he has destroyed himself, and
then he will hate the sins he loved before, flee from his false refuges,
forsake his joys, and seek to find a lasting salvation where alone it can
be found—in the blood of Christ.

The Voice of God Bemoaning Man's Lost Estate

Some have even ventured to translate the Hebrew, "Alas for thee,
alas for thee!" It is as if God uttered the words of the prophet, "How can
I give thee up? how can I utterly destroy thee? how can I set thee as
Admah? how shall I make thee as Zeboim? My repentings are kindled,
my bowels are moved for thee. Where art thou my poor Adam? Thou
didst talk with me, but thou hast now fled from me. Thou wast happy
once, what art thou now? Naked and poor and miserable. Thou was once
in my image glorious, immortal, blessed, where art thou now, poor
Adam? My image is marred in thee; thine own Father's face is taken
away, and thou hast made thyself earthy, sensual, devilish. Where art
thou, poor Adam?" Oh, it is wonderful to think how the Lord felt for
poor Adam. It is taken for granted by all theologians that God can neither feel nor suffer. There is no such thing in the Word of God. If it
could be said that God could not do anything and everything, we should
say that He was not omnipotent; but He can do all things, and we have
not a God that cannot be moved, but we have one who feels and who de-
scribes Himself in human language as having a father's compassion and
all the tenderness of a mother's heart. Just as a father cries over a rebellious son, so does the eternal Father say, "Poor Adam, where art thou?"

And now have I here this morning any soul on whom the former part of the text has had some effect? Do you feel yourself to be lost, and do you discern that this God bemoans you? He is looking down upon you and He is saying, "Ah, poor drunkard, why will you cling to your cups? Into what misery have they brought you?" He is saying to you who are now weeping over sin, "Ah, poor child, what pain you suffer from your own willful folly!" A father's is moved by compassion; he longs to clasp his Ephraim to his breast. Do not think, sinner, that God is stony-hearted. *You* have a heart of stone, God has not. Do not think that He is slow to move. *You* are slow to move—*He* is not; the hardness is in yourself. If you are straitened anywhere, it is in your own being, not in Him. Soul, soul convinced of sin! God loves you, and to prove He loves you, in the person of His Son He weeps over you, and He cries, "O that thou hadst known, even thou in this thy day, the things that make for thy peace; but now are they hid from thine eyes." I hear Him saying to you, "O Jerusalem, Jerusalem, how often would I have gathered thy children together as a hen gathereth her chickens under her wings, but ye would not!" I pray you, let this mournful wailing voice of the Eternal God come to your ear and move you to repentance! "As I live, saith the Lord, I have no pleasure in the death of him that dieth, but had rather that he would turn unto me and live."

Oh! does your heart feel ready to burst because of your sin and the misery into which it has brought you? Say, poor sinner, "I will arise and go unto my Father, and will say unto him, Father, I have sinned against heaven and in thy sight, and am no more worthy to be called thy son." He sees you, sinner; when you are yet a great way off, he sees you; here are *eyes* of mercy! He runs; here are *feet* of mercy! He clasps you; here are *arms of* mercy! He kisses you; here are *lips* of mercy! He says, "Take off his rags"; here are *words* of mercy! He clothes you; here are *deeds* of mercy! Wonders of mercy—all mercy! O did you know what a reception a God of mercy gives to sinners, you would not be long in going. As John Bunyan says, when the besieger hangs out the black flag, then those within the walls say they will fight it out; but when He runs up the white flag, and tells them that if they will open the gates He will have mercy upon them, no, He will give a charter to their city, then, says he, they say, "Fling open the gates," and they come tumbling over the walls to Him in the readiness of their hearts. Soul, let not Satan deceive you by telling you that God is hard, unkind, unwilling to forgive! Try Him, try Him! Just as you are—black, filthy, self-condemned; and if you need anything to make you try Him, hear again the Lord's plaintive cry as it rings through the trees of Eden, "Adam, poor Adam, my own creature, where, where art thou?"

The Voice of God Is a Seeking Voice

But now I must turn, lest time should fail us, to a fourth way in which no doubt this verse was intended. It is an arousing voice, a convincing voice, a bemoaning voice; but, in the fourth place, it is a seeking voice. "Adam, where art thou?" I am come to find thee, wherever you may be. I will look for you until the eyes of My pity see you, I will follow you until the hand of my mercy reaches you; and I will still hold you until I bring you back to Myself and reconcile you to My heart.

Again, if you have been able to follow me through the three parts of the discourse, I can speak confidently to you. If you have been aroused, if you have been convinced, if you have some longings toward God, then the Lord has come forth to seek you and to seek you this morning. What a thought it is, that when God comes forth to His chosen He knows where they are, and He never misses them; and though they may have wandered ever so far, yet it is not too far for Him. If they had gone to the gates of hell, and the gates were half opened to receive them, the Lord would get them even there. If they had so sinned that they had given themselves up, and every Christian living had given them up too—if Satan had counted upon them, and had made ready to receive them, yet when God comes forth to seek them He will find them, and He will have them after all. You who are lost, perishing sinners, hear the voice of God, for it speaks to you. "Where art thou?" for I am come to seek you. "Lord, I am in such a place that I cannot do anything for myself." "Then I am come to seek you and do all for you." "Lord, I am in such a place that the law threatens me and justice frowns upon me." "I am come to answer the threatenings of the law, and to bear all the wrath of justice." "But, Lord, I am in such a place that I cannot repent as I would." "I am come to seek you, and I am exalted on high to give repentance and remission of sins." "But, Lord, I cannot believe in You, I cannot believe as I would." "A bruised reed I will not break, and a smoking flax will I not quench; I am come to give you faith." "But, Lord, I am in such a state that my prayers can never be acceptable." "I am come to pray for you, and then to grant you your desires." "But, Lord, You do not know what a wretch I am." "Yes, I know you. Though I asked you the question, 'Where art thou?' it was that *you* might know where you are, for *I* knew well enough." "But, Lord, I have been the chief of sinners; none can have so aggravated their guilt as I have." "But wherever you may be I have come to save you." "But I am an outcast from society." "But I am come to gather together the outcasts of Israel." "Oh, but I have sinned beyond all hope." "Yes, but I have come to give hope to hopeless sinners." "Aye, but then I deserve to be lost." "Yes, but I have come to magnify the law and make it honorable, and so to give you your deserts in the person of Christ, and then to give you

My mercy because of *His* merits." There is not a sinner here conscious of his lost estate who can be in a position out of which he cannot be brought. I will conceive the worst of all the worst, the vilest of all the vile; we will bring up those who have taken high degrees in the Devil's synagogue and become masters of iniquity; but still if with the tearful eye they look alone to the wounds of Him who shed His blood for sinners, He is able to save them to the uttermost that come to God by Him.

Oh! I cannot preach this morning as I would, nor can you perhaps hear as you would wish; but may the Lord speak where I cannot, and may He say to some despairing sinner here, "Soul, my hour is come; I will pluck you out of the horrible pit and out of the miry clay, and this day, and at this very hour, I will set your feet upon a rock, I will put a new song into your mouth, and I will establish your goings." Blessed, blessed be the name of the Most High, is such may be the case.

The Voice of God Is the Voice of Justice Summoning Them

And now, lastly, we feel sure that this text may be used, and must be used, in another sense. To those who reject the text as a voice of arousing and conviction, to those who despise it as the voice of mercy bemoaning them or as the voice of goodness seeking them, it comes in another way; it is the voice of justice summoning them. Adam had fled, but God must have him come to His judgment. "Where art thou, Adam? Come hither, man, come hither; I must judge you, sin cannot go unpunished. Come, and your guilty spouse with you. Come hither; I must put questions to you; I must hear your pleadings, and since they will be vain and void I must pronounce your sentence." For though there was much of pity in the question, there was something of severity too. "Adam, Adam, where are you?" "Come you hither to be judged."

Today you hear not that cry; it is mercifully postponed. You shall hear it soon; you shall hear it for the first time, like mutterings of thunder when the storm begins, when sickness casts you on your bed and death looks through his bony eyes upon you and touches you with his ghastly hand and says, "Prepare to meet your God." You may put off the question today; you will have to deal with it then, when God Himself shall come into closer contact with your nature than He does today. Then shall your bones be as jelly, and your ribs shall quake, and your very heart shall melt like wax in the midst of your bowels. You shall contend with the pains of sickness or disease; but there shall be a direr pain than all your terrors, for you shall see behind death the judgment and the doom. *Then* you will hear it, when the room is silent and voices of wife and child are hushed; when only the clock is ticking, you shall hear the footfalls of God coming to you in the eventide of your life and saying to you, "Where are you? Now you shall meet Me. Gird up your loins! No invitations of mercy for you more; your day of mercy is gone. No warnings from the minister again; now you shall meet *Me* face-to-face." "Where art thou?"

Can you brag and boast now, when your nerves have become roads for the hot feet of pain to travel on, and your strength has gone and fled, and you are as a candle ready to die out? Where now your oaths? Where now your merry-makings and your jests? Where are you now? You may toss and turn, but you will be compelled to look forward to the life or the death to come, and still will the Lord whisper into your ears, "Where art thou? Where art thou?" Then shall come the last struggle, when the strong man shall be bowed, when the bright and glittering eye shall be covered over with film and the tongue shall cleave to the roof of the mouth and the hand shall lie strengthless on the bed and the feet shall no more be able to support the body, when the pulse shall fail and the clammy death-sweat shall stand upon the brow. In those last moments there will still be heard that awful voice, rising with the gathering storm until it reaches the full grandeur of the awful tempest— "Where art thou?"—in the Jordan without God; nearing the grave without hope; dying, but no Christ to help you; launching upon eternity, but no hope of eternal salvation. It is over; and the last pang has passed and the thread is snapped that bound the spirit to the body, and you are gone into another world. But the question follows you—"Where art thou?"

Your spirit is now awake; it sleeps no more; it is rid of the dull flesh that kept it sullen, stolid, stupid, dead. Now it hears that voice, indeed, and it thrills through and through the spirit, for the soul is brought before its God. "Where art thou? where art thou?" cries the quickened conscience; and God answers it, "Depart, thou cursed one!" The spirit departs from God, not to hide itself among the trees of the garden but to plunge itself into waves of agony. And now many years have passed, and the body, though the soul has been alive and has suffered, has been sleeping in the grave, and the worms have devoured it. But hark! the day of judgment, the day of thunder has arrived, shrill above all thunders sounds the awful trump; and after the trumpet comes the voice— "Awake, ye dead, and come to judgment!" Amid that awful tumult is heard the cry, "Where art *thou*?" The angelic messenger has found out *your* body, and from the grave your body starts from underneath the green sward. Up it leaps in answer to the question, "Where art thou?" and to its horror, its ghastly spirit comes back; its soul, that long has suffered, returns into the resurrection body, and they twain, comrades in sin, are now companions in judgment. The cry rings forth once more, and that very ear shall hear it that now listens to me—"Where art thou?" Then comes the great white throne, and those very eyes shall see it that now gaze on me; and then comes the commencement of the dread assize—and that heart shall quail then which moves not now. Then shall come your own personal trial; and oh! sinner, sinner, it is not for me to describe your terror, I could not give even the faintest picture of that death-sound and of the death of your immortal spirit while you hear it: "I was an hungered and ye gave me no meat; I was thirsty and ye gave me no drink; inasmuch as ye did it not unto one of the least of those my brethren ye did it not to me; and these shall go away into everlasting punishment, but the righteous into life eternal."

"Oh, earth! earth! earth! hear the word of the Lord," I pray each of you to hear it for yourselves. I have not talked to you of dreams; You know they are realities; and if you know it not now, you shall before long. I do beseech you by the blood of Him that died for sinners—and what stronger argument can I use?—think of the question, "Where art thou?" May God show you where you are. Hear the bemoaning voice of God, as pityingly he weeps over you. Seek His face, for He seeks you; and then you need not dread to hear Him say at the last, "Where art thou?" but you will be able to say, "Here am I and the children thou hast given me. We have washed our robes and made them white in the blood of the Lamb; and, Father, here we are, hoping to dwell in thy presence for ever and ever." Oh, that I could plead with you as a man pleads for his life! Would that these lips of clay were lips of fire, and this tongue no more of flesh, but a live coal taken with the tongs from off the altar! Oh! for words that would burn their way into your souls! O sinner, sinner, why will you die? Why will you perish? Man, eternity is an awful thing, and an angry God is a dreadful thing, and to be judged and condemned, what tongue can tell the horror. Escape for your life; look not behind you; stay not in all the plain; escape to mount Calvary, lest you be consumed. "Believe on the Lord Jesus Christ"; trust Him with your soul; trust Him with it now, "and thou shalt be saved, and thy house."

2

Enoch

And Enoch lived sixty and five years, and begat Methuselah: and Enoch walked with God after he begat Methuselah three hundred years, and begat sons and daughters: and all the days of Enoch were three hundred sixty and five years: and Enoch walked with God: and he was not; for God took him (Genesis 5:21–24).

By faith Enoch was translated that he should not see death; and was not found, because God had translated him: for before his translation he had this testimony, that he pleased God. But without faith it is impossible to please him: for he that cometh to God must believe that he is, and that he is a rewarder of them that diligently seek him (Hebrews 11:5–6).

And Enoch also, the seventh from Adam, prophesied of these, saying, Behold, the Lord cometh with ten thousands of his saints, to execute judgment upon all, and to convince all that are ungodly among them of all their ungodly deeds which they have ungodly committed, and of all their hard speeches which ungodly sinners have spoken against him (Jude 14–15).

The three passages of Scripture which I have read are all the authentic information we have concerning Enoch, and it would be idle to supplement it with the fictions of ancient commentators. Enoch is called the seventh from Adam, to distinguish him from the other Enoch of the line of Cain, who was the third from Adam. In the first patriarchs God was pleased to manifest to men portions of the truth in reference to true religion. These men of the olden times were not only themselves taught of God, but they were also teachers of their age and types in whom great truths were exhibited. Abel taught the need of

---

This sermon was taken from *The Metropolitan Tabernacle Pulpit* and was preached on Sunday morning, July 30, 1876.

approaching the Lord with sacrifice, the need of atonement by blood; he laid the lamb upon the altar and sealed his testimony with his own blood. Atonement is so precious a truth that to die for its defense is a worthy deed, and from the very first it is a doctrine which has secured its martyrs, who being dead yet speak.

Then Seth and Enos taught men the necessity of a distinct avowal of their faith in the Lord and the need of assembling for His worship, for we read concerning the days of Enos and Seth, "Then began men to call upon the name of the Lord." Those who worshiped through the atoning sacrifice separated themselves from the rest of men, assembled as a church in the name of the Lord, and worshiped, calling upon the name of Jehovah. The heart must first believe in the great sacrifice with Abel, and then the mouth must confess the same with Seth. Then came Enoch whose life went beyond the reception and confession of the atonement, for he set before men the great truth of communion with God; he displayed in his life the relation of the believer to the Most High and showed how near the living God condescends to be to His own children. May our progress in knowledge be similar to the growth of the patriarchal teaching. Brethren, you do know, as Abel did, the sacrificial lamb; your confidence is in the precious blood, and so by faith you bring to God the most acceptable of all offerings. Having advanced so far, the most of us have proceeded a step further, and we have called upon the name and are the avowed followers of Jesus. We have given ourselves up to the Lord in the solemn burial of baptism, when we were baptized into the name of the Father and of the Son and of the Holy Spirit, because we reckoned ourselves dead in Christ to all the world and risen with Him into newness of life. Henceforth the divine name is named on us, and we are no more our own. And now we gather together in our church capacity; we assemble around the table of fellowship; we unite in our meetings for prayer and worship, and the center for us all is the name of the Lord. We are separated from the world and set apart to be a people who declare His name. Thus far well we have seen the sacrifice of Jesus as *the way* with Abel; and we have avowed *the truth* with Seth; now let us take the next step and know *the life* with Enoch. Let us endeavor to walk with God as Enoch did.

Perhaps a meditation upon the holy patriarch's life may help us to imitate it; while considering what he was and under what circumstances he came to be so, we may by the Holy Spirit be helped to reach the point to which he attained. This is the desire of every godly man; all the saints desire communion with the Father and with His Son Jesus Christ. The constant cry of our soul is to our Lord, "Abide with me." I buried yesterday one of the excellent of the earth, who loved and feared and served his God far better than most of us; he was an eminently devout brother, and one of the last wishes of his heart he had committed to writing in a letter to a friend, when he little thought of dying. It was this: "I have longed to realize the life of Enoch, and to walk with God"—

Oh for a closer walk with God!

He did but write what you and I also feel. If such be your desires, and such I feel sure they are, so surely as you are the Lord's people, then I hope a consideration of the life of Enoch may help you toward the realization of your wish.

First, then, *what does Enoch's walking with God imply?* It is a short description of a man's life, but there is a mint of meaning in it; secondly, *what circumstances were connected with his remarkable life?* for these are highly instructive; and thirdly, *what was the close of it?* It was as remarkable as the life itself.

What Is Meant by Enoch's Walking with God?

Paul helps us to our first observation upon this by his note in the Hebrews. His walk with God was a testimony that *Enoch was well pleasing to God.* "Before his translation he had this testimony, that he pleased God." This is evidently the apostle's interpretation of his walking with God, and it is a most correct one, for the Lord will not walk with a man in whom He has no pleasure. Can two walk together, except they be agreed? If men walk contrary to God, He will not walk *with* them, but contrary to them. Walking together implies amity, friendship, intimacy, love, and these cannot exist between God and the soul unless the man is acceptable to the Lord. Doubtless Enoch, like Elias, was a man of like passions with ourselves. He had fallen with the rest of mankind in the sin of Adam; there was sin about him as there is sin about us by nature, and he had gone astray in act and deed as all we like sheep have done; therefore he needed pardon and cleansing, even as we do. Then to be pleasing with God it was needful that he should be forgiven and justified, even as we are; for no man can be pleasing to God until sin is pardoned and righteousness is imputed. To this end there must be faith, for there can be no justification except by faith, and as we have said already, there is no pleasing God except our persons are justified. Right well, then, does the apostle say, "Without faith it is impossible to please God," and by faith Enoch was made pleasing to God, even as we are at this day.

This is worthy of earnest notice, brethren, because this way of faith is open to us. If Enoch had been pleasing to God by virtue of some extraordinary gifts and talents or by reason of marvelous achievements and miraculous works, we might have been in despair; but if he was pleasing to God through faith, that same faith which saved the dying thief, that same faith which has been wrought in you and in me, then the wicket gate at the head of the way in which men walk with God is open to us also. If we have faith, we may enter into fellowship with the Lord. How this ought to endear faith to us! The highest grades of spiritual life depend upon the lower ones and rise out of them. If you want to walk with God as a man of God, you must begin by believing in the Lord Jesus Christ, simply, as a babe in grace. The highest saintship must commence by the confession of our sinnership and our laying hold upon Christ crucified. Not otherwise does the strongest believer live than the weakest believer; and if you are to grow to be among the strongest of the Lord's warriors, it must be by faith which lays hold upon divine strength. Beginning in the Spirit you are not to be made perfect in the flesh; you are not to proceed a certain distance by faith in Christ and then to commence living by your own works; your walk is to continue as it began. "As ye have received Christ Jesus the Lord so walk ye in him." Enoch was always pleasing to God, but it was because he always believed and lived in the power of his faith. This is worth knowing and remembering, for we may yet be tempted to strive for some imaginary higher style of religious life by looking to our feelings instead of looking alone to the Lord. We must not remove our eye from looking alone to Jesus Himself even to admire His image within ourselves; for if we do so, we shall go backward rather than forward. No, beloved; by faith Enoch became pleasing to God, and by faith he walked with God. Let us follow in his track.

Next, when we read that Enoch walked with God, we are to understand that *he realized the divine presence.* You cannot consciously walk with a person whose existence is not known to you. When we walk with a man, we know that he is there; we hear his footfall if we cannot see his face; we have some very clear perception that there is such a person at our side. Now, if we look to the Hebrews again, Paul tells us, "He that cometh to God must believe that he is, and that he is the rewarder of them that diligently seek him." Enoch's faith, then, was a realizing faith. He did not believe things as a matter of creed and then put them up on the shelf out of the way as too many do. He was not merely orthodox in head, but the truth had entered into his heart, and what he believed was true to him, practically true, true as a matter of fact in his daily life. He walked with God. It was not that he thought of God merely that he speculated about God, that he argued about God, that he read about God, that he talked about God, but he *walked* with God, which is the practical and experimental part of true godliness. In his daily life he realized that God was with him, and he regarded Him as a living friend in whom he confided and by whom he was loved. Oh, beloved, do you not see that if you are to reach to the highest style of Christian life, you must do it through the realization of those very things which by faith you have received? Grasp them, let them be to you substance and evidence. Make them sure, look upon them, handle them, taste them in your inmost soul, and so know them beyond all question. You must see Him who is invisible and possess that which cannot be as yet enjoyed. Believe not only that God is but that He is the rewarder of them that diligently seek Him, for this, according to Paul, is the Enoch faith—God realized as existing, observing, judging, and re-warding human deeds, a real God, really with us—this we must know, or there is no walking with God.

Then, as we read that Enoch walked with God, we have no doubt it signifies that *he had a very familiar relationship* with the Most High. I scarcely know a relationship that is more free, pleasant, and cordial than that which arises out of constant walking with a friend. If I wished to find a man's most familiar friend, it would surely be one with whom he daily walked. If you were to say, "I sometimes go into his house and sit a little while with him," it would not amount to so much as when you can say, "I have from day to day walked the fields and climbed the hills with him." In walking, friends become communicative—one tells his trouble, and the other strives to console him under it and then im-parts to him his own secret in return. When persons are constantly in the habit of walking together from choice, you may be quite sure there are many communications between them with which no stranger may intermeddle. If I wanted to know a man through and through, I should want to walk with him for a time, for walking communion brings out parts of the man which even in domestic life may be concealed. Walking for a continuance implies and engenders close fellowship and great familiarity between friends. But will God in very deed thus walk with men? Yes, He did so with Enoch, and He has done so with many of His people since. He tells us His secret, the secret of the Lord, which He reveals only to them that fear Him, and we tell to Him alike our joys in praise, our sorrows in prayer, and our sins in confession. The heart unloads itself of all its cares into the heart of Him that cares for us, and the Lord pours forth His floods of goodness as He imparts to the beloved ones a sense of His own everlasting love to them. This is the very flower and sweetness of Christian experience, its lily and its rose, its calamus and myrrh. If you would taste the cream of Christian life, it is found in having a realizing faith and entering into intimate relation-ship with the heavenly Father. So Enoch walked with God.

Next it is implied in the term "walked" that *his relationship with God was continuous*. As an old divine has well remarked, he did not take a turn or two with God and then leave His company, but he walked with

God for hundreds of years. It is implied in the text that this was the tenor of his life throughout the whole of its three hundred and sixty-five years. Enoch walked with God after Methuselah had been born, three hundred years, and doubtless he had walked with Him before. What a splendid walk! A walk of three hundred years! One might desire a change of company if he walked with anybody else, but to walk with God for three centuries was so sweet that the patriarch kept on with his walk until he walked beyond time and space and walked into paradise, where he is still marching on in the same divine society. He had heaven on earth, and it was therefore not so wonderful that he glided away from earth to heaven so easily. He did not commune with God by fits and starts, but he abode in the conscious love of God. He did not now and then climb to the heights of elevated piety and then descend into the marshy valley of lukewarmness; but he continued in the calm, happy, equable enjoyment of fellowship with God from day to day. Night with its sleep did not suspend it; day with its cares did not endanger it. It was not a run, a rush, a leap, a sport, but a steady *walk*. On, on, through three happy centuries and more did Enoch continue to walk with God.

It is implied also in this phrase that *his life was progressive*, for if a man walks either by himself or with anybody else, he makes progress; he goes forward. Enoch walked with God. At the end of two hundred years he was not where he began; he was in the same company, but he had gone forward in the right way. At the end of the third hundred years Enoch enjoyed more, understood more, loved more, had received more, and could give out more, for he had gone forward in all respects. A man who walks with God will necessarily grow in grace and in the knowledge of God and in likeness to Christ. You cannot suppose a perpetual walk with God year after year without the favored person being strengthened, sanctified, instructed, and rendered more able to glorify God. So I gather that Enoch's life was a life of spiritual progress; he went from strength to strength and made headway in the gracious pilgrimage. May God grant us to be pressing onward ourselves.

Suffer a few more observations upon Enoch's walk. In "Kitto's Daily Bible Readings" there is an exceedingly pleasing piece, illustrating what it must be to walk with God by the figure of a father's taking his little son by the hand and walking forth with him upon the breezy hills. He says, "As the child walks with thee, so do thou walk with God. That child loves thee now. The world—the cold and cruel world—has not yet come between his heart and thine. His love *now* is the purest and most beautiful he will ever feel, or thou wilt ever receive. Cherish it well, and as that child walks *lovingly* with thee, so do thou walk *lovingly* with God." It is a delight to such children to be with their father. The roughness of the way or of the weather is nothing to them: it is joy

enough to go for a walk with father. There is a warm, tender, affection-
ate grip of the hand and a beaming smile of the eye as they look up to
father while he conducts them over hill and dale. Such a walk is *humble*
too, for the child looks upon his father as the greatest and wisest man
that ever lived. He considers him to be the incarnation of everything
that is strong and wise, and all that his father says or does he admires.
As he walks along he feels for his father the utmost affection, but his
reverence is equally strong. He is very near his father, but yet he is only
a child and looks up to his father as his king.

Moreover such a walk is one of *perfect confidence*. The boy is not
afraid of missing his way; he trusts implicitly his father's guidance. His
father's arm will screen him from all danger, and therefore he does not
so much as give it a thought—why should he? If care is needed as to
the road, it is his father's business to see to it, and the child, therefore,
never dreams of anxiety—why should he? If any difficult place is to be
passed, the father will have to lift the boy over it or help him through it;
the child meanwhile is merry as a bird—why should he not be? Thus
should the believer walk with God, resting on eternal tenderness and rejoicing in undoubted love. A believer should be unconscious of dread
either as to the present or to the future. Beloved friend in Christ, your
Father may be trusted, He will supply all your need.

> Thou art as much his care as if beside
> No man or angel lived in heaven or earth.

What an *instructive* walk a child has with a wise, communicative
parent! How many of his little puzzles are explained to him; how
everything about him is illuminated by the father's wisdom. The boy
every step he takes becomes the wiser for such companionship. Oh,
happy children of God, who have been taught of their Father while they
have walked with Him! Enoch must have been a man of profound
knowledge and great wisdom as to divine things. He must have dived
into the deep things of God beyond most men.

His life must also have been a *holy* life, because he walked with
God, and God never walks out of the way of holiness. If we walk with
God, we must walk according to truth, justice, and love. The Lord has
no company with the unjust and rebellious, and therefore we know that
he who walked with God must have been an upright and holy man.

Enoch's life must, moreover, have been a *happy* one. Who could be
unhappy with such a companion! With God Himself to be with us the
way can never be dreary. "Yea, though I walk through the valley of the
shadow of death I will fear no evil, for thou art with me." Granted that
God is your companion, your road must be a way of pleasantness and a
path of peace.

Did Enoch walk with God, then his pilgrimage must have been *safe*. What a guard is the Great Jehovah! He is sun and shield; and glory. He that dwells in the secret place of the Most High shall abide under the shadow of the Almighty. Nothing can harm the man who is walking with the Lord God at his right hand.

And oh, what an honorable thing it is to walk with the Eternal! Many a man would give thousands to walk with a king. Numbers of people are such worshipers of dignities that if a king did but smile at them they would be intoxicated with delight. What, then, is the honor of walking with the King of Kings! What a patent of nobility it is to be permitted to walk with the blessed and only Potentate all one's life long! Who is he that is thus favored to be the King's companion, to walk alone with Him, and to become His familiar friend? Jehovah rules earth and heaven and hell and is Lord of all who shall walk with *Him!* If it were only for the honor of it, oh Christians, how you ought to pant to walk with God. Enoch found it safe, happy, holy, honorable, and I know not how much more that is excellent, but certainly this was a golden life. Where shall we find anything to equal it?

What Circumstances Were Connected
with Enoch's Walking with God?

The first remark is that the details of his life are very few. We do not know much about Enoch, and this is to his advantage. Happy is the nation which has no history, for a nation which has a history has been vexed with wars and revolutions and bloodshed; but a nation that is always happy, peaceful, and prosperous has no chronicle to attract the lover of sensations. Happy is Enoch that we cannot write a long biography of him; the few words, "Enoch walked with God," suffice to depict his whole career, until "he was not, for God took him." If you go and look at a farmer's field, and you can say of it when you come back, "I saw yellow flowers covering it until it seemed a cloth of gold, and then I spied out here and there white flowers like silver buttons set on the golden vesture, and blue corn-flowers also looked up with their lovely eyes and begemmed the whole," you will think that it is a very pretty field if you are a child; but the farmer shakes his head, for he knows that it is in bad condition and overrun with weeds; but if you come back and simply say, "It is as fine a piece of wheat as ever grew, and that is all," then your description, though brief, is very satisfactory.

Many of those dazzling events and striking incidents and sensational adventures which go to make up an interesting biography may attract attention, but they do not minister to the real excellence of the life. No life can surpass that of a man who quietly continues to serve God in the place where providence has placed him. I believe that in the judgment of angels and all pure-minded beings that woman's life is most to be admired which consists simply of this: "*She did what she could*"; and that man's life shall be the most noteworthy of whom it can be said: "*He followed the Lord fully.*" Enoch's life has no adventures; is it not adventure enough for a man to walk with God? What ambition can crave a nobler existence than abiding in fellowship with the Eternal?

But some will say, "Well, but Enoch must have been very peculiarly situated. He was no doubt placed in very advantageous circumstances for piety." Now, observe that this was not so, for first, *he was a public man*. He is called the "seventh from Adam." He was a notable man and looked up to as one of the fathers of his age. A patriarch in those days must have been a man of mark, loaded with responsibility as well as with honor. The ancient custom was that the head of the family was prophet, priest, and king in his household, and abroad if he was a man of station and substance, he was counselor, magistrate and ruler. Enoch was a great man in his day, one of the most important of the period; hence we may be sure he had his trials and bore the brunt of opposition from the powerful ungodly party which opposed the ways of godliness. He is mentioned among a noble list of men. Some have unwisely thought, "I could walk with God if I had a little cottage, if I lived in a quiet village, but you see I am a public man, I occupy a position of trust, and I have to mix with my fellow men. I do not see how I am to walk with God." Ah, my dear friend, but Enoch did; though he was undoubtedly a man distinguished in his time and full of public cares, yet he lost not the thread of sacred converse with heaven but held on in his holy course through a life of centuries.

Note again that *Enoch was a family man.* "Enoch walked with God and begat sons and daughters." Some have said, "Ah, you cannot live as you like if you have a lot of children about you. Do not tell me about keeping up your hours of prayer and quiet reading of the Scriptures if you have a large family of little ones; you will be disturbed, and there will be many domestic incidents which will be sure to try your temper and upset your equanimity. Get away into the woods and find a hermit's cell, there with your brown jug of water and your loaf of bread you may be able to walk with God, but with a wife, not always amiable, and a troop of children who are never quiet, neither by day nor night, how can a man be expected to walk with God?" The wife on the other hand exclaims, "I believe that had I remained a single woman I might have walked with God. When I was a young woman I was full of devotion, but now with my husband, who is not always in the best of tempers, and with my children, who seem to have an unlimited number of wants and never to have them satisfied, how is it possible that I can walk with God?" We turn to Enoch again, and we are confident that it can be done. "Enoch walked with God after he begat Methuselah three hundred years, and begat sons and daughters, and all the days of Enoch were three hundred and sixty-five years." Thus, you see, he was a public man, and he was a family man, and yet he walked with God for more than three hundred years. There is no need to be a hermit or to renounce the married life in order to live near to God.

In addition to this, Enoch lived in a very evil age. He was prominent at a time when sin was beginning to cover the earth, not very long before the earth was corrupt and God saw fit to sweep the whole population from off its surface on account of sin. Enoch lived in a day of mockers and despisers. You know that from his prophecy, as recorded by Jude. He prophesied, saying, "The Lord cometh with ten thousands of his saints, to execute judgment upon all, and to convince all that are ungodly among them of all their ungodly deeds which they have ungodly committed, and of all their hard speeches which ungodly sinners have spoken against him." He lived when few loved God and when those who professed to do so were being drawn aside by the blandishments of the daughters of men. Church and state were proposing an alliance, fashion and pleasure ruled the hour, and unhallowed compromise was the order of the day. He lived toward the close of those primitive times wherein long lives had produced great sinners, and great sinners had invented great provocations of God. Do not complain, therefore, of your times and of your neighbors and other surroundings, for amid them all you may still walk with God.

Enoch walked with God, and in consequence thereof *he bore his witness for God.* "Enoch the seventh from Adam prophesied." He could not be silent; the fire burned within his soul and could not be restrained. When he had delivered his testimony, it is clear that he encountered opposition. I am certain that he did so from the context in Jude, because the passage in Jude has to do with murmurers and "complainers, walking after their own lusts; and their mouth speaketh great swelling words," and Enoch is brought in as having had to do with such persons. His sermon shows that he was a man who stood firm amidst a torrent of blasphemy and rebuke, carrying on the great controversy for the truth of God against the wicked lives and licentious tongues of the scoffers of his age; for he says, "Behold, the Lord cometh with myriads of his saints, to execute judgment upon all, and to convince all that are ungodly among them of all their ungodly deeds which they have ungodly committed." It is clear that they spoke against Enoch; they rejected his testimony; they grieved his spirit, and he mourned that in this they were speaking against God; for he speaks "of all their hard speeches which ungodly sinners have spoken against him." He saw their ungodly lives and bore witness against them. It is remarkable that his great subject should have been the second advent, and it is still more noteworthy that the two other men whom one would select as living nearest to God, namely, Daniel and John, were both men who spoke much concerning the coming of the Lord and the great judgment day. I need not quote the words of Daniel, who tells us of the judgment which is to be set and of the Ancient of Days who shall come upon His throne; nor need I repeat the constant witness of John concerning the Lord's second coming, I will only mention his fervent exclamation, "Even so, come quickly, Lord Jesus."

Thus you see that Enoch was a preacher of the Word of God, and therefore he had a care over and above that which falls to the lot of most of you. Yet with that and all the rest put together he could please God until his life's end, if I may speak of an end to a life which ran into an endless state of joy. He continued as long as he was here to walk in faith, to walk in a manner in which God was pleased, and so his communion with the Lord was never broken.

What Was the Close of Enoch's Walk?

We would first remark that *he finished his work early*. Enoch walked with God, and that was such a good, sure, progressive walk that he traveled faster and reached his house sooner than those of us who walk with God sometimes and with the world at other times. Three hundred and sixty-five years would have been a long life to us, but it was a short life for that period when several patriarchs attained to nearly a thousand years of age. Enoch's life as compared to the usual life of the period was like a life of thirty or thirty-five years in these short-lived ages—in fact, the best parallel to it is the life of our Lord. As compared with the extended ages of men of his period, Enoch's life was of about the same length as that of the Lord Jesus in comparison with such lives as ours. He passed away comparatively a young man, as our dear brother and elder Verdon, just departed, has done; and we do not wonder that he did. They say "Whom the gods love die young." Both Enoch and Verdon were men greatly beloved. Perhaps these holy men ended their career so soon because they had done their life-work so diligently that they finished betimes. Some workmen, if they have a job to do in your house, are about it all day long, or rather all the week long, and make no end of chips and confusion. No wonder that some people live a long while, for they had need to do so to do anything at all! But this man did his work so well and kept so close to God that his day's work was done at noon, and the Lord said, "Come home, Enoch, there is no need for you to be out of heaven any longer; you have borne your testimony; you have lived your life; through all the ages men will look upon you as a model man, and therefore you may come home." God never keeps

His wheat out in the fields longer than is necessary; when it is ripe, He reaps it at once. When His people are ready to go home, He will take them home. Do not regret the death of a good man while he is young; on the contrary, bless God that still there is some early ripening wheat in the world and that some of His saints are sanctified so speedily.

But what did happen to Enoch? I am afraid I have said he died, or that I shall say so; it is so natural to speak of men as dying, but he alone and one other of all the human race are all that have entered the heavenly Canaan without fording the river of death. We are told concerning him that "he was not." Those gentlemen who believe that the word to "die" signifies to be annihilated would have been still more confirmed in their views if the words in my text, "he was not" had been applied to all departed men, for if any expression might signify annihilation on their mode of translation—this is the one. "He was not" does not, however, mean that he was annihilated, and neither does the far feebler term of dying signify anything of the kind. "He was not"; that is to say, he was not here, that is all. He was gone from earth, but he was there, there where God had translated him. He was, he is with God, and that without having tasted death. Do not grudge him his avoidance of death. It was a favor, but not by any means so great as some would think, for those who do not die must undergo a change, and Enoch was changed. "We shall not all sleep," says the apostle Paul, "but we shall all be changed." The flesh and blood of Enoch could not inherit the kingdom of God. In a moment he underwent a transformation which you and I will have to undergo in the day of the resurrection; and so, though he was not on earth, he was translated or transplanted from the gardens of earth to the paradise above. Now, if there is any man in the world that shall never die, it is he who walks with God. If there is any man to whom death will be as nothing, it is the man who has looked to the second advent of Christ and gloried in it; if there is any man who, though he pass through the iron gates of death shall never feel the terror of the grim foe, it is the man whose life below has been perpetual communion with God. Go not about by any other way to escape the pangs of death, but walk with God, and you will be able to say, "O death, where is thy sting? O grave, where is thy victory?"

It is said of him that "*God took him.*" A very remarkable expression. Perhaps he did it in some visible manner. I should not wonder. Perhaps the whole of the patriarchs saw him depart even as the apostles were present when our Lord was taken up. However that may be, there was some special rapture, some distinct taking up of this choice one to the throne of the Most High. "He was not, for God took him."

Note that *he was missed*. This is one thing which I could not overlook. *He was missed*, for the apostle says he "was not found." Now, if a man is not found, it shows that somebody looked after him. When Elijah went to heaven, you remember fifty men of the sons of the prophets went and searched for him. I do not wonder that they did; they would not meet with an Elijah every day, and when he was gone away, body and all, they might well look for him. Enoch was not found, but they looked after him. A good man is missed. A true child of God in a church like this, working and serving his Master, is only one among five thousand; but if he has walked with God, his decease is lamented. The dear brother whom we have just buried we shall miss; his brother elders will miss him; the many who have been converted to God and helped by his means will miss him, and assuredly I shall miss him. I look toward the spot where he used to sit—I trust that someone else will sit there who will be half as useful as he was; it will be almost more than I can expect. We do not want so to live and die that nobody will care whether we are on earth or not. Enoch was missed when he was gone, and so will they be who walk with God.

Last of all, *Enoch's departure was a testimony*. What did he say by the fact that "he was not, for God took him," but this: there is a future state? Men had begun to doubt it, but when they said, "Where is Enoch?" and those who had witnessed his departure said, "God took him," it was to them an evidence that there was a God and that there was another world. And when they said, "But where is his body?" there was another lesson. Two men had died before him, I mean two whose deaths are recorded in Scripture—Abel was killed, and his witness was that the seed of the serpent hates the woman's seed; Adam, too, had died about fifty years before Enoch's translation, whose witness was that, however late the penalty may come, yet the soul that sins shall die. Now comes Enoch, and his testimony is that the body is capable of immortality. He could not bear testimony to resurrection, for he did not die. For that we have testimony in Christ, who is the first fruits from among the dead; but the testimony of Enoch went a good way toward it, for it bore evidence that the body was capable of being immortal and of living in a heavenly condition. "He was not, for God took him."

His departure also was a testimony to mankind that there is a reward for the righteous, that God does not sit with stony eyes regardless of the sins of the wicked or of the virtues of His saints, but that He sees and is pleased with His people who walk with Him and that He can give them even now present rewards by delivering them from the pangs of death, and therefore He will certainly give rewards to all His people in some way or other. Thus you see, living and dying—no, not dying, again I do mistake—living and being translated, Enoch was still a witness to his generation, and I do pray that all of us, whether we live or whether we sleep, may be witnesses for God. Oh that we could live as my good brother Verdon, whom we have lately buried, lived, whose soul was on fire with love to Christ. He had a very passion for souls. I scarcely think there is one among us who did as much as he, for though he had to earn his daily bread, his evenings were spent with us in the service of the Lord or in preaching the Gospel. Then all night long he frequently paced the weary streets looking after the fallen that he might bring them in and often went to his morning's work unrested, except by the rest which he found in the service of Christ. He would sometimes meet a brother with eyes full of joy and say, "Five souls won for Christ last night." At other times after a sermon here he was a great soul hunter and would fetch inquirers downstairs into the prayer meeting, and when he had squeezed my hand he would say in his Swiss tones, which I cannot imitate, "Jesus saved some more last night; more souls were brought to Jesus." For him to live was to win souls. He was the youngest in our eldership, but the gray-heads do him honor. As we stood weeping about his tomb, there was not one among us but what felt that we had lost a true brother and a valiant fellow-soldier. The Lord raise up others among you to do what Elder Verdon did! The Lord quicken the elder brethren to be more active than they are and make the young ones more devoted. Our ranks are broken; who shall fill up the gap? We are getting fewer and fewer as the Lord takes one and another home of the best instructed and of the bravest hearted, but recruits are daily coming in. May others come forward—yes, Lord, bring them forward by Your Holy Spirit to be leaders in the front rank, that as the vanguard melts into the church triumphant, the rear may continually find additions. Translated to the skies are some, may others be translated out of darkness into marvelous light, for Christ's sake. Amen.

3

Jacob Worshiping on His Staff

By faith Jacob, when he was a dying, blessed both the sons of Joseph; and worshiped, leaning upon the top of his staff (Hebrews 11:21).

W hen he was a dying." Death is a thorough test of faith. Beneath the touch of the skeleton finger shams dissolve into thin air, and only truth remains; unless indeed a strong delusion has been given, and then the spectacle of a presumptuous sinner passing away in his iniquities is one which might make angels weep. It is hard, very hard, to maintain a lie in the presence of the last solemnities; the end of life is usually the close of self-deception. There is a mimic faith, a false assurance, which lasts under all ordinary heats of trial, but this evaporates when the fires of death surround it. Certain men are at peace and quiet in their conscience; they stifle convictions; they refuse to allow such a thing as self-examination; they count an honest self-suspicion to be a temptation of the Devil and boast of their unbroken tranquillity of mind and go on from day to day with perfect confidence; but we would not be of their order. Their eyes are closed; their ears are dull of hearing, and their heart has waxen gross. A siren song forever enchants them with delight but also entices them to destruction. Terrible will be their awakening when they lie a dying; as a dream their false peace will vanish, and real terrors will come upon them. That expression, "When he was a dying," reminds me of many deathbeds; but I shall not speak of them now, for I desire each one of you to rehearse the scene of his own departure, for soon of everyone a tale will be told commencing—"When he was a dying."

This sermon was taken from *The Metropolitan Tabernacle Pulpit* and was preached at the Metropolitan Tabernacle, Newington, in 1878.

34

I want each one to project his mind a little forward to the time when he must gather up his feet in the bed, pronounce his last farewell, and yield up the ghost. Before your actual departure, probably, there may be allotted to you, unless you are carried away with a sudden stroke, a little time in which it shall be said, "He was a dying." Perhaps it is a desirable thing to occupy some weeks in departure, until the mind seems to have passed through the gate and to be already in the glory, while yet the body lingers here; but as we have had no experience, we are scarcely able to form a judgment. Very much might be said in favor of that sudden death which is sudden glory, but yet one might prefer to have enough time and sufficient clearness of mind to gaze into eternity and so to become familiar with the thought of departing out of the body. It would seem desirable to lose the dread and first surprise of the chill torrent and to become fully at ease on the banks of Jordan, sitting with your feet up to the ankles in its stream and by degrees descending into the greater depths, singing, singing, singing, singing, and beginning even on earth the everlasting song which is heard forever on the other side of the mysterious river. Such dying is a fit ending to a life of genuine piety and both displays and proves its truthfulness. Jacob was a dying, and in his dying we see the man.

The text tells us that the patriarch's faith was firm while he was a dying, so that he poured forth no murmurs, but plentiful benedictions, as he blessed both the sons of Joseph. May your faith and mine also be such that whenever we shall be a dying, our faith will perform some illustrious exploit that the grace of God may be admired in us. Paul does not say anything about Jacob's life, but selects the death scene. There were many instances of faith in Jacob's life story, but you recollect that in the epistle to the Hebrews Paul is walking through the histories and plucking a flower here and a flower there, and he complains that time fails him even in doing that, so fertile is the garden of faith. I do not doubt, however, that he gathered the best out of each biography; and, perhaps, the finest thing in Jacob's life was the close of it. He was more royal between the curtains of his bed than at the door of his tent, greater in the hour of his weakness than in the day of his power. Some days are damp and foggy from morning until late in the afternoon, but just before the sun goes down there is a calm, bright hour, and the sun sets in such glory that you forget the gloom of the day. Albeit that all the former part of the day was commonplace enough, yet the closing hour is at times so gorgeous in splendor that you recollect the day for its sunset and mark it down in your diary as a memorable date. Jacob's death has certainly so much of glorious faith in it that the apostle did well to select it for special record.

The old man of one hundred and forty-seven might have been willing to depart through infirmities of age, but yet he had much to keep him below and make him wish to live as long as possible. After a very troublous life he had enjoyed seventeen years of remarkable comfort, so much so that, had it been ourselves, we should probably have begun to strike our roots into the soil of Goshen and dread the bare thought of removal; yet there sits the venerable patriarch with his hand on his staff ready to go, seeking no delay, but rather waiting for the salvation of God. After all his tossings to and fro when he had been so long a pilgrim, it must have been a pleasant thing for him to have settled down in a fat land with his sons and his grandsons and great-grandsons all around him, all comfortably provided for, with Joseph at the head of the whole country—prime minister of Egypt—reflecting honor upon his old father and taking care that none of the family wanted anything. The last course of Jacob's feast of life was by far the sweetest, and the old man might have been loath to retire from so dainty a table.

The children of Israel were a sort of foreign aristocracy in the land, and against them would not a dog dare to move its tongue, lest the renowned Joseph should put forth his hand. That seventeen years must have been bright and full of rest to the old man. But sense has not killed his faith; luxury has not destroyed his spirituality; his heart is still in the tents where he had dwelt as a sojourner with God. You can see that he has not even with one single rootlet of his soul taken hold upon Egypt. His first anxiety is to take care that not even his bones shall lie in Goshen but that his body shall be taken out of the country as a protest to his family that they are not Egyptians and cannot be made into subjects of Pharaoh and that Canaan is their possession to which they must come. By his dying charge to bury him in Machpelah he practically teaches his descendants that they must set loose by all the good land which they possessed in Goshen, for their inheritance did not lie on the banks of the Nile but on the other side of the desert in Canaan, and they must be on tiptoe to journey thither. The blessing which he gave to the sons of Joseph was but an utterance of his firm faith in the covenant which gave the land to him and to his seed. It was suggested by that faith of his which let go the present and grasped the future, renounced the temporal and seized the eternal, refusing the treasures of Egypt and clinging to the covenant of God.

Three things are brought before us by the text. The first is *the blessing*; the second is *the worshiping*; and the third is *the attitude*; for he "worshiped, leaning upon the top of his staff," which must be significant, or else it would not have been recorded.

Jacob's Blessing

He blessed the two sons of Joseph. Will you have patience with me while I try to show that his blessing the sons of Joseph was an act of faith, because, first, only by faith could the old man really give a blessing to any one? Look at him. He is too feeble to leave his bed. When he sits up supported by pillows at what is called the bed-head, he calls for his trusty staff that he may lean upon it while he raises himself up a little to be in a position to stretch out his hands and to use his voice. He has no strength, and his eyes are dim, so that he cannot see which is Ephraim and which is Manasseh. He is failing in most of his faculties; every way you can see that he is a worn-out old man who can do nothing for the children whom he loves. If he is able to bestow a blessing, it cannot be by the power of nature; and yet he can and does bless them, and therefore we feel sure that there must be an inner man within that feeble old Jacob; there must be a spiritual Israel hidden away in him, an Israel who by prevailing with God as a prince has obtained a blessing and is able to dispense it to others. And so there is, and at half a glance we see it.

He rises to the dignity of a king, a prophet, and a priest when he begins to pronounce a blessing upon his two grandchildren. He believed God. He believed that God spoke by him, and he believed that God would justify every word that he was uttering. He believed in the God that hears prayer; his benediction was a prayer; and as he pronounced blessings upon his grandsons, he felt that every word he was speaking was a petition which the Lord was answering. They were blest, and they should be blest, and he discerned it by faith. Thus, we see, he was manifesting his faith in offering believing prayer and in uttering a confident benediction.

Dear friends, whether we live or whether we die, let us have faith in God; whenever we preach or teach the Gospel, let us have faith; for without faith we shall labor in vain. Whenever you distribute religious books or visit the sick, do so in faith, for faith is the life-blood of all our service. If only by faith can a dying Jacob bless his descendants, so only by faith can we bless the sons of men. Have faith in God, and the instruction which you give shall really edify, the prayers you offer shall bring down showers of mercy, and your endeavors for your sons and daughters shall be prospered. God will bless what is done in faith; but if we believe not, our work will not be established. Faith is the backbone and marrow of the Christian's power to do good. We are weak as water until we enter into union with God by faith, and then we are omnipotent. We can do nothing for our fellowmen by way of promoting their spiritual and eternal interests if we walk according to the sight of our eyes; but when we get into the power of God and grasp His promise by daring confidence, then it is that we obtain the power to bless.

You will notice, also, that *not only the power to bless came to him by*

faith, but the blessings which he allotted to his grandsons were his
upon the same tenure. His legacies were all blessings which he possessed by faith only. He gave to Ephraim and Manasseh a portion each,
but where and what? Did he fetch out a bag from the iron safe and say,
"Here, young men, I give you the same portion of ready money as I
give my sons"? No, there does not seem to have been a solitary shekel
in the case. Did he call for the map of the family estates and say, "I give
over to you, my boys, my freehold lands in such a parish and my copy-
hold farms under such a manor"? No, no, he gave them no portion in
Goshen, but each had a lot in Canaan.

Did that belong to him? Yes, in one sense, but not in another. God
had promised it to him, but he had not yet a foot of land in it. The
Canaanites were swarming in the land; they were dwelling in cities
walled up to heaven and held the country by the right of possession,
which is nine points of the law. But the good old man talks about
Canaan as if it was all his own, and he foresees the tribes growing into
nations as much as if they were already in actual possession of the
country. He had, as a matter of fact, neither house nor ground in
Palestine, and yet he counts it all his own, since a faithful God had
promised it to his fathers. God had said to Abraham, "Lift up now thine
eyes and behold to the east and to the west, to the north and to the
south. All this will I give thee." And Jacob realizes that gift of God as
being a charter and title-deed of possession, and he acts upon it while
he says, "This is for Ephraim: this is for Manasseh," though the sneering infidel standing by would have said, "Hear how the old man dotes
and maunders, giving away what he has not got!" Faith is the substance
of things hoped for, and she deals seriously and in a business manner
with that which she makes real to herself; blind reason may ridicule,
but faith is justified of all her children.

Beloved, in this manner believers bless the sons of men, namely, by
faith. We pray for them, and we tell them of good things yet to come,
not to be seen of the eye or to be perceived by the senses, but incon-
ceivably good—things laid up by God for them that love Him, which
shall be the portion of our children and our friends if they believe in the
living God. By faith we believe in things not seen as yet. We confess
that, like Abraham, Isaac, and Jacob, we are strangers here, and we are
journeying toward a place of which God has spoken to us—"A city
which hath foundations, whose builder and maker is God." We have
learned to talk about the crown which the Lord has laid up for us, and
not for us only but for all them that love His appearing; and we delight
to tell others how to win this crown. We point them to the narrow gate
and to the narrow way, neither of which they can see, and to the end of
that narrow road, even to the hilltops crowned with the celestial city

where the pilgrims of the Lord shall dwell forever and enjoy an eternal reward. Faith is wanted to enable us to point men to the invisible and eternal, and if we cannot do this, how can we bless them? We must believe for those we love and have hope for them; thus shall we have power with God for them and shall bless them. Oh, you worldly fathers, you may give your sons what heritage you can and divide among your daughters what wealth you please, but as for us, our longing is to see our children and our children's children dowried with the riches which come from above. If they win a share in the land on the other side of Jordan, as yet unseen, and have a portion now in Christ Jesus, we shall be glad—infinitely more glad than if they were the richest among mankind. Our legacies to our sons are the blessings of grace, and our dowries to our daughters are the promises of the Lord.

It is well worthy of our notice that *the venerable patriarch Jacob in his benediction particularly mentioned the covenant.* His faith, like the faith of most of God's people, made the covenant its pavilion of delightful abode, its tower of defense, and its armory for war. No sweeter word was on his tongue than the covenant, and no richer consolation sustained his heart. He said to Joseph, "God almighty appeared unto me at Luz in the land of Canaan, and blessed me, and said unto me, Behold I will make thee fruitful, and multiply thee." His confidence rested in the promise of the Lord and in the divine fidelity. That was the fountain truth from which he drew the inspiration which led him to bless his grandchildren. And, also, you notice, how he dwells upon the name of his father Abraham and of his father Isaac, with whom the covenant had aforetime been established. The memories of covenant love are precious, and every confirmatory token is treasured up and dwelt upon.

Dying men do not talk nonsense. They get to something solid, and the everlasting covenant made with their fathers and confirmed in their own persons has been one of the grand things about which dying saints have been wont to deliver their souls. Recollect how David said, "Although my house be not so with God, yet hath he made with me an everlasting covenant, ordered in all things and sure." While we are sitting here we can talk about the matter coolly, but when the death dew lies cold upon the brow and the pulse is failing and the throat is gradually choking up, it will be blessed to fix the eye upon the Faithful Promiser and to feel a calm within the soul which even death pangs cannot disturb, because we can then exclaim, "I know whom I have believed, and I am persuaded that he is able to keep that which I have committed to him until that day." My dear hearers, if you have no faith, you cannot plead the covenant, and certainly if you cannot plead it for yourselves, you cannot urge it with God for a blessing upon your sons and your grandsons. It was by faith in the covenant that the venerable Jacob blessed the two sons of Joseph, and without it we can bless no one, for we are not blessed ourselves. Faith is the priest which proclaims the blessing without fear.

> We pronounce our benediction
>   O'er our son's beloved head,
> For the promise is no fiction,
>   God will do what he has said.

> Covenant love and covenant blessing,
>   Cause our happy lips to bless,
> For by faith each boon possessing,
>   Our glad hearts can do no less.

I want to call your attention to one point which I think extraordinarily illustrates the faith of Jacob. In distributing to these two grandchildren his blessings as to the future, he takes them right away from Joseph and says, "As Simeon and Reuben shall they be mine." Do you know who those two young gentlemen were? Think awhile, and you will see that they were very different in rank, station, parentage, and prospects from any of the sons of Jacob. Jacob's sons had been brought up as laboring men, without knowledge of polite society or learned arts. They were countrymen, mere Bedouins, wandering shepherds, and nothing else; but these two young gentlemen were descended from a princess and had, no doubt, been liberally educated. Pharaoh had given to Joseph a daughter of Poti-pherah, priest of On, and the priests of Egypt were the highest class of all—the nobility of the land. Joseph himself was prime minister, and these were partakers of his lofty rank. The sons of Reuben and Simeon were nobodies in the polite circles of Egypt—very good, decent people, farmers and grazers, but not at all of the high class of the Right Honorable Lord Manasseh and the Honorable Ephraim. Indeed, every shepherd was an abomination to the Egyptians and therefore inadmissible to Egypt's nobility; but Manasseh and Ephraim were of a superior caste, and gentlemen of position and fortune.

But *Jacob showed his faith by ignoring worldly advantages for his grandsons.* He says to Joseph, "They are not to be yours. I do not know them as Egyptians; I forget all about their mother's rank and family. The boys have attractive prospects before them; they can be made priests of the idol temple and rise to high dignities among the Egyptians; but all that glitter we reject for them, and in token thereof I adopt them as my own sons; they are mine; as Simeon and Reuben they shall be mine. For all the gold of Egypt you would not have one of them serve an idol, for I know that you are true to your father's God and your father's faith." And so he takes the boys right away, you see, from all their brilliant opportunities and bestows upon them that which to the carnal mind appears to be an estate in dreamland, a chateau in Spain, something intangible and unmarketable.

This was a deed of faith, and blessed are they who can imitate it, choosing rather the reproach of Christ for their sons than all the treasures of Egypt. The joy of it is that these lads accepted the exchange and let the golden possessions of Egypt go like Moses after them. May our heirs and successors be of like mind, and may the Lord say of them, "Out of Egypt have I called my son"; and again, "When Ephraim was a child then I loved him, and called my son out of Egypt." This is how faith leads believers to bless their children. We are of the same mind as Jacob in this matter. We would sooner bury our little ones than that they should live to become among the richest and most famous of men and yet not know or serve their father's God. Better that we laid them quietly in such ground as our Christian brethren permit us to use as a sepulcher for our unbaptized babes, better that they were safely housed at God's right hand, than that they should grow up to plunge into dissipation or to follow false doctrine and perish out of Christ. Yes, yes, the good old man was content that his family should be as poor as he was in Canaan, so long as they might have a possession in the land of promise.

Do you not see, then, how by faith Jacob blessed the two sons of Joseph, putting aside their temporal prospects and bestowing upon them the blessing which belongs to the children of the promise?

We have not done yet, for we notice that *Jacob showed his faith by blessing Joseph's sons in God's order*. He placed Ephraim before Manasseh. It was not according to the rule of nature, but he felt the impulse upon him, and his faith would not resist the divine guidance. Blind as he was, he would not yield to the dictation of his son but crossed his hands to obey the divine monition. Faith resolves to do the right thing in the right way. Some persons' faith leads them to do the right thing the wrong way upward, but matured faith follows the order which God prescribes. If God will have Ephraim first, faith does not quarrel with His decree. We may wish to see a favorite child blessed more than another, but nature must forego her choice, for the Lord must do what seems Him good. Faith prefers grace to talent and piety to cleverness; she lays her right hand where God lays it and not where beauty of person or quickness of intellect would suggest. Our best child is that which God calls best; faith corrects reason and accepts the divine verdict.

Notice that *he manifested his faith by his distinct reference to redemption*. He alone who has faith will pray for the redemption of his children, especially when they exhibit no signs of being in bondage but are hopeful and amiable. The good old man prayed, "The Angel which

redeemed me from all evil, bless the lads." Let your faith bring down
upon your children a share in redemption's blessings, for they need to
be redeemed even as others. If they are washed in the blood of Jesus, if
they are reconciled to God by the blood of His Son, if they have access
to God by the blood of atonement, you may die well satisfied; for what
is to harm them when once the angel that redeemed you has also redeemed them? From sin, from Satan, from death, from hell, from self—
"from all evil" does our Redeemer set us free; and this is the greatest of
all benedictions which we can pronounce upon our dearest children.
Beloved hearers, thus would I pray for you—may the redeeming angel
deliver *you* from all evil.

*Jacob showed his faith by his assurance that God would be present
with his seed.* How cheering is the old man's dying expression, made not
only to his boys but concerning all his family. He said, "Now I die, but
God will be with you." It is very different from the complaints of certain
good old ministers when they are dying. They seem to say, "When I die,
the light of Israel will be quenched. I shall die, and the people will desert
the truth. When I am gone the standard-bearer will have fallen, and the
watchman on the walls will be dead." Many in dying are afraid for the
chariot of Israel and the horsemen thereof; and, sometimes, we who are
in good health talk very much in the same fashion as though we were
wonderfully essential to the progress of God's cause. I have known
some of our church members speak in that manner and inquire: "What
should we do if Mr. So-and-so were dead! If our pastor were gone, what
would the church do?" I will tell you what you will do without us. I will
put the case as though I were myself about to die—"Now I die, but God
will be with you." Whoever passes away, the Lord will abide with His
people, and the church will be secure. The grand old cause does not depend on one or two of us. God forbid! The truth was mighty in the land
before the best man living was born, and when he is carried with funeral
procession, sad and slow, to his resting place, the truth will not be buried
with him, but in its own immortal youth will still be powerful; yes, and
fresh advocates will arise more full of life and vigor than we are, and
greater victories will be won. If you cut down yonder noble oak which
now covers so wide an area with its shade, there may spring up a dozen
trees which else had been overshadowed by the giant and checked in
their growth. The removal of one man is often the opportunity for the
springing up of scores of others to do equal service. It is grand to say
with Jacob, "Now I die, but God will be with you." Such language honors God and bespeaks a mind greatly trustful and completely delivered
from the self-conceit which dreams itself important, if not necessary, to
the cause of God. So may we die trusting in the Lord, and meanwhile so
may we live, reliant upon the divine power.

Thus much about Jacob's benediction. By faith he blessed the two sons of Joseph.

Jacob's Worshiping

The old man worshiped by faith. This act no man can rightly perform without faith, for he that comes to God must believe that He is and that He is the rewarder of them that diligently seek Him. The point here is that he worshiped in his dying hour and worshiped in blessing his two grandsons. Very briefly let me tell you what worship I think he rendered.

First, while he was dying he offered the worship of *gratitude*. How pleasing is the incident recorded in the tenth and eleventh verses, "Now the eyes of Israel were dim for age, so that he could not see. And Joseph brought his two sons near unto him; and he kissed them and embraced them. And Israel said unto Joseph, I had not thought to see thy face: and, lo, God hath showed me also thy seed." Ah, yes, we shall often have to say, "O Lord, I had not thought that You would do as much as this, but You have gone far beyond what I asked or even thought." I hope that this will be among our dying speeches and confessions, that the half was never told us, that our good Lord kept the best wine until the last, and that the end of the feast on earth, being but the beginning of the feast eternal in heaven, was the crown of all. Let us declare concerning our Lord that we found Him better and better and better and better, even until we entered into His rest. He has been at first better than our fears, then better than our hopes, and finally better than our desires. So good, so blessed a God do we serve, that He always by His deeds of grace outruns our largest expectations. What cause we have for the worship of grateful praise; let us not be slow to render it. Jacob worshiped by expressions of gratitude.

Did he not also offer the worship of *testimony*, when he acknowledged God's goodness to him all his life? He says, "The God that fed me all my life long," thus owning that he had been always dependent but always supplied. He had been a shepherd, and he uses a word here which means "The God that shepherdized me—who was a shepherd to me all my life long." It was a testimony to the care and tenderness of Jehovah. Jacob does not murmur now and declare that all things are against him. Now he no longer quarrels and frets and makes rash declarations; now he does not even make a bargain with God, but he cries, "The God that fed me all my life long." Yes, and I hope we also shall finish life by magnifying the goodness of the Lord. Be this our witness, "He fed me all my life long. I was in straits sometimes, and I wondered where the next bit of bread would come from; but if He did not send a raven, or if He did not find a widow woman to provide for me, yet somehow or other He did feed me all my life long. He worked in His own wise way, so that I never lacked, for the Lord was my shepherd all my life long." Thus you see that Jacob worshiped by the testimony of faith when he came to die, and this is exceedingly acceptable with the Lord.

Notice, too, how reverently he worships the covenant messenger with the adoration of *reverent love*. He speaks of "the angel who redeemed me from all evil." He thinks of the angel that wrestled with him and the angel that appeared to him when he fell asleep at Bethel. This is *the* angel, not an ordinary angel, but the true *arch*angel—Jesus Christ— the messenger of the covenant whom we delight in. It is He that has delivered us from all evil by His redeeming blood, for no other being could have accomplished a redemption so complete. Do you remember when He came to you personally and wrestled with you and tore away your self-righteousness and made you limp upon your thigh? This it may be was your first introduction to Him. You saw Him by night and thought Him at the first to be rather your enemy than your friend. Do you recollect when He took your strength away from you and then at last saved you, because in utter weakness, as you were about to fall to the ground, you laid hold of Him and said, "I will not let thee go except thou bless me," and so you won a blessing from Him? You had thought aforetime that you had strength in yourself, but now you learned that you were weakness itself, and that only as you became consciously weak would you become actually strong. You learned to look out of self to Him, and do you not bless Him for having taught you such a lesson? Will you not when you come to die bless Him for what He did for you then and all your life long? O my brethren, we owe all things to the redeeming Angel of the covenant. The evils which He has warded off from us are terrible beyond conception, and the blessings He has brought us are rich beyond imagination. We must adore Him, and, though we see Him not, we must in life and in death by faith worship Him with lowly love.

If you read on through the dying scene of Jacob, you will notice once more how he worshiped with the adoration of *earnest longing*, for just after he had pronounced a blessing on the tribe of Dan the old man seemed thoroughly exhausted and gasped as if about to faint, but instead of fainting, instead of uttering a cry of pain and weakness, he solemnly exclaims, "I have waited for thy salvation, O Lord." It is a holy utterance interjected into the very middle of a prophecy—"I have waited for thy salvation, O God"; as much as to say, "I long to be gone. My heart is all with You. Make no tarrying, O my God. Strengthen me to get through this one more task of telling the future to my sons, and enable me to offer my last prayer for their welfare, and then, Lord, bring Your salvation.

> Come death and some celestial band
> To bear my soul away.

Thus you have had a picture of the old man blessing by faith, and worshiping by faith. Faith was the mainspring of the two actions, their essence, their spirit, and their crown.

Jacob's Attitude

He "worshiped leaning upon the top of his staff." The Romanists have made fine mischief out of this text, for they have read it, "He worshiped the top of his staff," and their notion has been, I suppose, that there was a pretty little god carved on the top—an image of a saint or a cross, or some other symbol and that he held up that emblem and so worshiped the top of his staff. We know that he did no such thing, for there is no trace in Abraham, Isaac, or Jacob of anything like the worship of images. Though teraph worship lingered in their families, it was not with their consent. They were not perfect men, but they were perfectly clear from idolatry and never worshiped an image. No, no, no; they worshiped God alone. He worshiped on the top of his staff—leaning on it, supporting himself upon it. In Genesis you read that he "bowed himself upon the bed's head." It is a very curious thing that the word for bed and the word for staff in the Hebrew are so exceedingly like each other that unless the little points had been used, which I suppose were not used at all in the olden time, it would be difficult to tell whether the word is "bed" or "staff." I do not, however, think either Moses or Paul can be wrong. Jacob strengthened himself and sat upon the bed, and he leaned upon his staff, too. It is very easy to realize a position in which both descriptions would be equally true. He could sit upon the bed and lean on the top of his staff at the same time.

But why did he lean on his staff? What was that for? I think besides the natural need which he had of it, because of his being old, he did it emblematically. Do you not remember his saying, "With my staff I crossed this Jordan"? I believe he kept that staff throughout life as a memorial. It was a favorite staff of his which he took with him on his first journey, and he leaned upon it as he took his last remove. "With my staff I crossed this Jordan," he had said before, and now with that staff in hand he crosses the spiritual Jordan. That staff was his life companion, the witness with himself of the goodness of the Lord, even as some of us may have an old Bible or a knife or a chair which are connected with memorable events of our lives.

But what did that staff indicate? Let us hear what Jacob said at another time. When he stood before Pharaoh he exclaimed, "Few and evil have been the days *of my pilgrimage.*" What made him use that word

"pilgrimage"? Why, because upon his mind there was always the idea
of his being a pilgrim. He had been literally so during the early part of
his life, wandering hither and thither; and now, though he has been seventeen years in Goshen, he keeps the old staff, and he leans on it to
show that he had always been a pilgrim and a sojourner like his fathers
and that he was so still. While he leans on that staff he talks to Joseph,
and he says, "Do not let my bones lie here. I have come hither in the
providence of God, but I do not belong here. This staff indicates that I
am only a sojourner here and want to be gone. I am in Egypt, but I am
not of it. Take my bones away. Do not let them lie here, for if they do,
my sons and daughters will mingle with the Egyptians and that must
not be, for we are a distinct nation. God has chosen us for Himself, and
we must keep separate. To make my children see this, lo, here I die
with my pilgrim staff in my hand." "Give me my staff," the old man
seems to say, "I will die with it in my hand. I protest that I am not a res-
ident here, but only a lingerer for a little while. I will stay myself upon
it and for the last time worship God in the attitude of one who longs to
be up and away." Now, Christian brother, I want you to live in the same
spirit, feeling that this is not your rest nor your native country. There is
nothing here that is worthy of you. Your home is yonder, on the other
side the desert, where God has mapped out your portion. Christ has
gone to prepare your place, and it would ill become you to have no desires for it. The longer you live the more let this thought grow upon
you: "Give me my staff. I must be gone. Poor world, thou art no rest for
me; I am not of your children; I am an alien and a stranger. My citizen-
ship is in heaven. I take my share in Egypt's politics and Egypt's labor,
aye, and in Egypt's griefs, but I am no Egyptian; I am a stranger bound
for another land." Worship on the top of your staff, and sing—

> A scrip on my back, and a staff in my hand,
>   I march on in haste through an enemy's land;
> There is nothing on earth which can tempt me to stay,
>   My staff is the emblem of "up and away."

Singular enough is it that each descendant of Jacob came to worship
on the top of his staff at last, for on the paschal supper night, when the
blood was sprinkled on the lintel and the side posts, they each one ate
the lamb with their loins girt and with a staff in his hand. The supper
was a festival of worship, and they ate it each one leaning on his staff,
as those that were in haste to leave home for a pilgrimage through the
wilderness.

Brethren and sisters, let us imitate Jacob in his dying faith. May the
Holy Spirit in the power of our Lord Jesus enable you to live by faith.
Live to bless others, especially your own descendants; live to worship

God at all times; and live with your hand on your staff, saying always, "This is not our rest, for it is polluted."

My dear hearers, this advice does not apply to all of you, for you are not all Jacobs, nor do you belong to the believing seed. I cannot bid you take your staff, for if you were to take your staff and start off, where would you go? You have no portion in the next world, no promised land, no Canaan flowing with milk and honey. Whither will you go? You must be banished from the presence of the Lord and from the glory of His power. Alas for you! You cannot worship, for you know not God; you cannot bless others, for you have not been blessed yourselves. May the Lord bring you to His dear Son Jesus Christ and lead you to put your trust in Him, and then I shall hope that being saved you will by faith imitate Jacob and both bless men, worship God, and wait with your staff in your hand, ready to journey to the eternal rest. The Lord be with you, for Christ's sake. Amen.

4

Moses' Decision

By faith Moses, when he was come to years, refused to be called the son of Pharaoh's daughter; choosing rather to suffer affliction with the people of God, than to enjoy the pleasures of sin for a season, esteeming the reproach of Christ greater riches than the treasures in Egypt: for he had respect unto the recompense of the reward (Hebrews 11:24–26).

Last Sabbath day we spoke upon the faith of Rahab. We had then to mention her former unsavory character and to show that, notwithstanding, her faith triumphed and both saved her and produced good works. Now, it has occurred to me that some persons would say, "This faith is, no doubt, a very suitable thing for Rahab and persons of that class; a people destitute of sweetness and light may follow after the Gospel, and it may be a very proper and useful thing for them, but the better sort of people will never take to it." I thought it possible that, with a sneer of contempt, some might reject all faith in God, as being unworthy of persons of a higher condition of life and another manner of education. We have, therefore, taken the case of Moses, which stands as a direct contrast to that of Rahab, and we trust it may help to remove the sneer; though, indeed, that may be of small consequence, for if a man is given to sneering, it is hardly worthwhile to waste five minutes in reasoning with him. The scorner is usually a person so inconsiderable that his scoffing deserves to be unconsidered. He who is great at sneering is good for nothing else, and he may as well be left to fulfill his vocation.

It occurred to me also that, perhaps, some might in all seriousness, say, "I have, through the providence of God and the circumstances which surround me, been kept from outward sin; moreover, I am not a

---

This sermon was taken from *The Metropolitan Tabernacle Pulpit* and was preached on Sunday morning, July 28, 1872.

member of the lowest ranks and do not belong to the class of persons of whom Rahab would be a suitable representative. In fact, I have, by the providence of God, been placed in a choice position and can, without egotism, claim a superior character." It is possible that such persons may feel as if they were placed under a disadvantage by this very superiority. The thought has passed over their mind, "The Gospel is for sinners; it evidently comes to the chief of sinners and blesses them. We are free to admit that we are sinners, but possibly, because we have not sinned so openly, we may not be so conscious of the sin, and consequently our mind may not be so well prepared to receive the abounding grace of God which comes to the vilest of the vile." I have known some who have almost wished that they were literally like the prodigal son in his wanderings, that they might be more readily like him in his return. It is altogether a mistake under which they labor, but it is by no means an uncommon one. Perhaps, as we introduce to their notice one of the heroes of faith who was a man of noble rank, high education, and pure character, they may be led to correct their thoughts. Moses belonged to the noblest order of men, but he was saved by faith alone, even by the same faith which saved Rahab. This faith moved him to the faithful service of God and to a self-denial unparalleled. My earnest prayer is that you who are moral, amiable, and educated, may see in the action of Moses an example for yourselves. No longer despise a life of faith in God. It is the one thing which you lack, the one thing above all others needful. Are you young men of high position? Such was Moses. Are you men of spotless character? Such also was he. Are you now in a position where to follow out conscience will cost you dear? Moses endured as seeing Him who is invisible, and though for a while a loser, he is now an eternal gainer by the loss. May the Spirit of God incline you to follow in the path of faith, virtue, and honor, where you see such a man as Moses leading the way.

We shall first consider *the decided action of Moses*; and, secondly, *the source of his decision of character*—it was "by faith." Thirdly, we shall look into *those arguments by which his faith directed his action*; after which we shall briefly reflect upon those practical lessons which the subject suggests.

The Decided Action of Moses

"When he had come to years he refused to be called the son of Pharaoh's daughter." We need not narrate the stories which are told by Josephus and other ancient writers with regard to the early days of Moses, such as for instance, his taking the crown of Pharaoh and trampling upon it. These things may be true; it is equally possible that they are pure fiction. The Spirit of God has certainly taken no notice of them in Holy Scripture, and what He does not think worth recording, we need not think worth considering. Nor shall I more than hint at answers to the question why it was that Moses remained no less than forty years in the court of Pharaoh and doubtless during that time was called "the son of Pharaoh's daughter" and, if he did not enjoy the pleasures of sin, at any rate, had his share in the treasures of Egypt.

It is just possible that he was not a converted man up to the age of forty. Probably during his early days he was to all intents and purposes an Egyptian, an eager student, a great proficient in Egyptian wisdom, and also, as Stephen tells us in the Acts, "a man mighty in words and in deeds." During those early days he was familiar with philosophers and warriors, and perhaps in his engrossing pursuits he forgot his nationality. We see the hand of God in his being forty years in the court of Pharaoh; whatever of evil or indecision in him may have kept him there, we see the good result which God brought out of it, for he became by his experience and observation the better able to rule a nation and a fitter instrument in the hand of God for fashioning the Israelitish slate into its appointed form. Perhaps during the forty years he had been trying to do what a great many are aiming at just now. He was trying whether he could not serve God and remain the son of Pharaoh's daughter too. Perhaps he was of the mind of our brethren in a certain church who protest against ritualism but still remain in that church which gives to ritualism the fullest liberty. Perhaps he thought he could share the treasures of Egypt and yet bear testimony with Israel. He would be known as a companion of the priests of Iris and Osiris and yet at the same time would bear honest witness for Jehovah. If he did not attempt this impossibility, others in all ages have done so. It may be he quieted himself by saying that he had such remarkable opportunities for usefulness that he did not like to throw them up by becoming identified with the Israelitish dissenters of the period. An open avowal of his private sentiments would shut him out from good society and especially from the court, where it was very evident that his influence was great and beneficial.

It is just possible that the very feeling which still keeps so many good people in a wrong place may have operated upon Moses until he was forty years of age; but then, having reached the prime of his manhood and having come under the influence of faith, he broke away from the ensnaring temptation, as I trust many of our worthy brethren will before long be able to do. Surely they will not always maintain a confederacy with the allies of Rome but will be men enough to be free. If when Moses was a child he spoke as a child and thought as a child, when he became a man, he put away his childish ideas of compromise. If, when he was a young man, he thought he might conceal a part of the truth and so might hold his position, when he came to ripe years enough to know what the truth fully was, he scorned all compromise and came out boldly as the servant of the living God.

The Spirit of God directs our eye to the time when Moses came to years. That is to say, when his first forty years of life were over; then, without any hesitation he refused to be called the son of Pharaoh's daughter and took his part with the despised people of God.

I beg you to consider first, *who he was that did this*. He was a man of education, for he was learned in all the wisdom of the Egyptians. Somebody says he does not suppose the wisdom of the Egyptians was anything very great. No, and the wisdom of the English is not much greater. Future ages will laugh as much at the wisdom of the English as we now laugh at the wisdom of the Egyptians. The human wisdom of one age is the folly of the next. Philosophy, so called, what is it but the concealment of ignorance under hard names and the arrangement of mere guesses into elaborate theories? In comparison with the eternal light of God's Word all the knowledge of men is "not light but darkness visible." Men of education, as a rule, are not ready to acknowledge the living God. Philosophy in its self-conceit despises the infallible revelation of the Infinite and will not come to the light lest it be reproved. In all ages, when a man has considered himself to be wise, he has almost invariably condemned the Infinite wisdom. Had he been truly wise, he would have humbly bowed before the Lord of all, but being only nominally so he said, "Who is the Lord?" Not many great men after the flesh, not many mighty are chosen. Did not our Lord Himself say it, and His word is for all time, "I thank thee, O Father, Lord of heaven and earth, that thou hast hid these things from the wise and prudent, and hast revealed them unto babes?" But yet, sometimes a man of education, like Moses, is led by the blessing of heaven to take the side of truth and of the right, and when it is so, let the Lord be magnified!

Beside being a man of education, he was a person of high rank. He had been adopted by Thermuthis, the daughter of Pharaoh, and it is possible, though we cannot be sure of it, that he was the next heir by adoption to the Egyptian crown. It is said that the King of Egypt had no other child and that his daughter had no son and that Moses would, therefore, have become the King of Egypt. Yet, great as he was and mighty at court, he joined with the oppressed people of God. May God grant that we may see many eminent men bravely standing up for God and for His truth and repudiating the religion of men. But if they do, it will be a miracle of mercy indeed, for few of the great ones have ever done so. Here and there in heaven may be found a king, and here and there in the church may be found one who wears a coronet and prays; but how hardly shall they that have riches enter into the kingdom of heaven. When they do so, God be thanked for it.

In addition to this, remember that Moses was a man of great ability. We have evidence of that in the administrative skill with which he managed the affairs of Israel in the wilderness; for though he was inspired of God, yet his own natural ability was not superseded but directed. He was a poet: "Then sung Moses and the children of Israel this song unto the Lord." That memorable poem at the Red Sea is a very masterly ode and proves the incomparable ability of the writer. The ninetieth Psalm also shows the range of his poetic powers. He was both prophet, priest, and king in the midst of Israel and a man second to no man save that Man who was more than man. No other man I know of comes so near in the glory of his character to Christ as Moses does, so that we find the two names linked together in the praise of heaven—"They sung the song of Moses the servant of God, and of the Lamb." Thus you see he was a truly eminent man, yet he cast in his lot with God's people. It is not many that will do this, for the Lord has usually chosen the weak things to confound the mighty and the things that are not to bring to nothing the things that are, that no flesh should glory in his presence. Yet here He, who will have mercy on whom He will have mercy, took this great man, this wise man, and gave him grace to be decided in the service of his God. Should I address such a one this morning I would anxiously pray that a voice from the excellent glory may call him forth to the same clear line of action.

Next, consider *what sort of society Moses felt compelled to leave.* In coming forth from Pharaoh's court he must separate from all the courtiers and men of high degree, some of whom may have been very estimable people. There is always a charm about the society of the great, but every bond was severed by the resolute spirit of Moses. I do not doubt that being learned in all the wisdom of Egypt, such a man as Moses would be always welcome in the various circles of science; but he relinquished all his honors among the *elite* of learning to bear the reproach of Christ. Neither great men nor learned men could hold him when his conscience had once pointed out the path. Be sure, also, that he had to tear himself away from many a friend. In the course of forty years one would suppose he had formed associations that were very dear and tender, but to the regret of many he associated himself with the unpopular party whom the king sought to crush, and therefore no courtier could henceforth acknowledge him. For forty years he lived in the solitude of the desert, and he only returned to smite the land of Egypt with plague, so that his separation from all his former friendships must have been complete. But, O true-hearted spirit, should it break every fond connection, should it tear your soul away from all you love, if your God requires it, let the sacrifice be made at once. If your faith has shown you that to occupy your present position involves complicity with error or sin, then break away, by God's help, without further parley. Let not the nets of the fowler hold you, but as God gives you freedom, mount untrammeled and praise your God for liberty. Jesus left the angels of heaven for your sake; can you not leave the best of company for His sake?

But I marvel most at Moses when I consider not only who he was and the company he had to forego, but *the persons with whom he must associate*, for in truth the followers of the true God were not, in their own persons, a lovable people at that time. Moses was willing to take upon himself the reproach of Christ and to bear the affliction of God's people when, I venture to observe again, there was nothing very attractive in the people themselves. They were wretchedly poor; they were scattered throughout all the land as mere drudges, engaged in brick making, and this brick making, which was imposed upon them for the very purpose of breaking down their spirit, had done its work all too well. They were utterly spiritless; they possessed no leaders and were not prepared to have followed them if they had arisen. When Moses, having espoused their cause, informed them that God had sent him, they received him at first, but when the prophet's first action prompted Pharaoh to double their toil by an enactment that they should not be supplied with straw, they upbraided Moses at once; even as forty years before, when he interfered in their quarrels, one of them said, "Wilt thou slay me as thou didst the Egyptian yesterday?" They were literally a herd of slaves, broken down, crushed, and depressed.

It is one of the worst things about slavery that it unmans men and unfits them even for generations for the full enjoyment of liberty. Even when slaves receive liberty, we cannot expect them to act as those would do who were free born, for in slavery the iron enters into the very soul and binds the spirit. Thus it is clear that the Israelites were not very select company for the highly educated Moses to unite with. Though a prince, he must make common cause with the poor; though a free man, he must mingle with slaves; though a man of education, he must mix with ignorant people; though a man of spirit, he must associate with spiritless serfs. How many would have said, "No, I cannot do that; I know what church I ought to unite with if I follow the Scriptures fully and obey in all things my Lord's will. But then they are so poor, so illiterate, and their place of worship is so far from being architecturally beautiful. Their preacher is a plain, blunt man, and they themselves are not refined. Scarce a dozen of the whole sect can keep a carriage. I should be shut out of society if I joined with them." Have we not heard this base reasoning until we are sick of it, and yet it operates widely upon this brainless, heartless generation. Are there none left who love truth even when she wears no trappings? Are there none who

love the Gospel better than pomp and show? Where God raises up a
Moses, what cares he how poor his brethren may be? "They are God's
people," says he, "and if they are very poor, I must help them the more
liberally. If they be oppressed and depressed, so much the more reason
why I should come to their aid. If they love God and His truth, I am
their fellow-soldier and will be at their side in the battle." I have no
doubt Moses thought all this over, but his mind was made up, and he
took his place promptly.

In addition to other matters, one mournful thing must be said of
Israel, which must have cost Moses much pain. He found that among
God's people there were some who brought no glory to God and were
very weak in their principles. He did not judge the whole body by the
faults of some, but by their standards and their institutions; and he saw
that the Israelites, with all their faults, were the people of God, while
the Egyptians, with all their virtues, were not so. Now, it is for each one
of us to try the spirits by the Word of God and then fearlessly to follow
out our convictions. Where is Christ recognized as the head of the
church? Where are the Scriptures really received as the rule of faith?
Where are the doctrines of grace clearly believed? Where are the ordinances practiced as the Lord delivered them? For with that people will I
go; their cause shall be my cause; their God shall be my God. We look
not for a perfect church this side of heaven, but we do look for a church
free from sacramentarianism and false doctrine; and if we cannot find
one, we will wait until we can, but with falsehood and priestcraft we
will never enter into fellowship. If there be faults with the brethren, it is
our duty to bear with them patiently and pray for grace to overcome the
evil; but with Papists and Rationalists we must not join in affinity, or
God will require it at our hands.

Consider now *what Moses left by siding with Israel.* He left honor—
he refused to be called the son of Pharaoh's daughter." He left pleasure—for he refused to "enjoy the pleasures of sin for a season." And,
according to our apostle, he left wealth as well, for in taking up the reproach of Christ he renounced "the treasures of Egypt." Very well,
then, if it comes to this, if to follow God and to be obedient to Him I
have to lose my position in society and become a pariah, if I must abjure a thousand pleasures, and if I am deprived of emoluments and in-
come, yet the demands of duty must be complied with. Martyrs gave
their lives of old, are there none left who will give their livings? If there
be true faith in a man's heart, he will not deliberate which of the two to
choose, beggary or compromise with error. He will esteem the reproach
of Christ to be greater riches than the treasures of Egypt.

Consider yet once more *what Moses espoused* when he left the
court. He espoused abounding trial, "choosing rather to suffer affliction

with the people of God"; and he espoused reproach, for he "esteemed the reproach of Christ greater riches than the treasures of Egypt." O, Moses, if you must need join with Israel, there is no present reward for you; you have nothing to gain but all to lose; you must do it out of pure principle, out of love to God, out of a full persuasion of the truth, for the tribes have no honors or wealth to bestow. You will receive affliction, and that is all. You will be called a fool, and people will think they have good reason for so doing. It is just the same today. If any man today will go without the camp to seek the Lord, if he go forth to Christ without the gate, he must do it out of love to God and to his Christ and for no other motive. The people of God have no benefices or bishoprics to offer; they therefore beseech men to count the cost. When a fervent convert said to our Lord, "Lord I will follow thee whithersoever thou goest," he received for an answer, "Foxes have holes and the birds of the air have nests, but I, the Son of Man, have not where to lay my head." To this hour truth offers no dowry but herself to those who will espouse her. Abuse, contempt, hard fare, ridicule, misrepresentation— these are the wages of consistency; and if better comes, it is not to be reckoned on. If any man be of a noble enough spirit to love the truth for truth's sake and God for God's sake and Christ for Christ's sake, let him enlist with those of like mind; but if he seek anything over and above that, if he desire to be made famous or to gain power or to be well beneficed, he had better keep his place among the cowardly dirt-eaters who swarm around us. The church of God bribes no man. She has no mercenary rewards to proffer and would scorn to use them if she had. If to serve the Lord is not enough reward, let those who look for more go their selfish way. If heaven is not enough, let those who can despise it seek their heaven below. Moses, in taking up with the people of God, decidedly and once for all, acted most disinterestedly, without any promise from the right side or any friend to aid him in the change; for the truth's sake, for the Lord's sake, he renounced everything, content to be numbered with the down-trodden people of God.

The Source of Moses' Decision

What was the source of Moses' decision? Scripture says it was faith; otherwise some would insist upon it that it was the force of blood. "He was by birth an Israelite, and therefore," say they, "the instincts of nature prevailed." Our text assigns a very different reason. We know right well that the sons of godly parents are not led to adore the true God by reason of their birth. Grace does not run in the blood; sin may, but righteousness does not. Who does not remember sons of renowned lovers of the Gospel who are now far gone in Ritualism? It was faith, not blood, which impelled Moses in the way of truth. Neither was it eccentricity which led him to espouse the side which was oppressed. We have sometimes found a man of pedigree and position who has associated with persons of quite another rank and condition, simply because he never could act like anybody else and must live after his own odd fashion. It was not so with Moses. All his life through you cannot discover a trace of eccentricity in him. He was sober, steady, law-abiding; what if I say he was a *con*centric man, for his center was in the right place, and he moved according to the dictates of prudence. Not thus can his decision be accounted for. Neither was he hurried on by some sudden excitement when there burned within his soul fierce patriotic fires which made him more fervent than prudent. No, there may have been some haste in his slaying the Egyptian on the first occasion, but then he had forty more years to think it over, and yet he never repented his choice but held on to the oppressed people of God and still refused to think of himself as the son of Pharaoh's daughter. It was faith then, faith alone, that enabled the prophet of Sinai to arrive at his decision and to carry it out.

What faith had he? First, he had faith in Jehovah. It is possible that Moses had seen the various gods of Egypt, even as we see them now in the drawings which have been copied from their temples and pyramids. We find there the sacred cat, the sacred ibis, the sacred crocodile, and all kinds of creatures which were reverenced as deities; and in addition there were hosts of strange idols, compounded of man and beast and bird, which stand in our museums to this day and were once the objects of the idolatrous reverence of the Egyptians. Moses was weary of all this symbolism. He knew in his own heart that there was one God, one only God, and he would have nothing to do with Amun, Pthah, or Maut. Truly, my very soul cries to God that noble spirits may in these days grow weary of the gods of ivory and ebony and silver, which are adored under the name of crosses and crucifixes, and may come to abominate that most degrading and sickening of all idolatries in which a man makes a god with flour and water, bows down before it, and then swallows it, thus sending his god into his belly, and, I might say worse. The satirist said of the Egyptians, "O happy people, whose gods grow in their own gardens"; we may say with equal force, O happy people, whose gods are baked in their own ovens! Is not this the lowest form of superstition that ever debased the intellect of man. O that brave and true hearts may be led to turn away from such idolatry and abjure all association with it and say, "No, I cannot and dare not. There is one God that made heaven and earth; there is a pure Spirit who upholds all things by the power of His might; I will worship Him alone; and I will worship Him after His own law, without images or other symbols, for has He not forbidden them." Has He not said, "Thou shalt not make unto thee any graven image, or any likeness of anything that is in heaven above, or that is in the earth beneath, or that is in the water under the earth: thou shalt not bow down thyself to them, nor serve them: for I the Lord thy God am a jealous God"? Oh that God would give to men faith to know there is but one God and that the one God is not to be worshiped with man-ordained rites and ceremonies, for He is "a Spirit, and they that worship Him must worship Him in spirit and in truth!" That one truth, if it were to come with power from heaven into men's minds, would shiver St. Peter's and St. Paul's from their topmost cross to their lowest crypt. For what do these two churches teach us now but sheer clear idolatry, the one of rule and the other by permission, for now men who boldly worship what they call the "sacred elements" have leave and license to exercise their craft within the Church of England. Every man who loves his God should shake his skirts clear of these abominations, and I pray God that we may find many a Moses who shall do so.

The faith of Moses also rested in Christ. "Christ had not come," says one. No, but He was to come, and Moses looked to that coming One. He cast his eye through the ages that were to intervene, and he saw before him the Shiloh of whom dying Jacob sang. He knew the ancient promise which had been given to the fathers, that in the seed of Abraham should all the nations of the earth be blessed; and he was willing, in order to share in the blessing, to take his part in the reproach. Dear Friends, we shall never have a thorough faith in God unless we have also faith in Jesus Christ. Men have tried long, and tried hard, to worship the Father apart from the Son; but there stands it, and it always will be so: "No man cometh unto the Father but by me." You get away from the worship of the Father if you do not come through the mediation and atonement of the Son of God. Now, though Moses did not know concerning Christ all that is now revealed to us, yet he had faith in the coming Messiah, and that faith gave strength to his mind. Those are the men to suffer who have received Christ Jesus the Lord. If any man should ask me what made the Covenanters such heroes as they were, what made our Puritanic forefathers fearless before their foes, what led the Reformers to protest and the martyrs to die, I would reply, it was faith in the Invisible God coupled with faith in that dear Son of God who is God Incarnate. Believing in Him, they felt such love within their bosoms that for love of Him they could have died a thousand deaths.

But then, in addition to this, Moses had faith in reference to God's people. Upon that I have already touched. He knew that the Israelites were God's chosen, that Jehovah had made a covenant with them, that despite all their faults, God would not break His covenant with His own people. He knew, therefore, that their cause was God's cause, and being God's cause, it was the cause of right, the cause of truth. Oh, it is a grand thing when a man has such faith that he says, "It is nothing to me what other people do or think or believe; I shall act as God would have me. It is nothing to me what I am commanded to do by my fellow creatures, nothing to me what fashion says, nothing to me what my parents say as far as religion is concerned. The truth is God's star, and I will follow wherever it may lead me. If it should make me a solitary man, if I should espouse opinions which no one else ever believed in, if I should have to go altogether outside the camp and break away from every connection, all this shall be as immaterial to me as the small dust of the balance; but if a matter is true, I will believe it, and I will propound it, and I will suffer for its promulgation; and if another doctrine is a lie, I will not be friends with it, no, not for a solitary moment; I will not enter into fellowship with falsehood, no, not for an hour. If a course be right and true, through floods and flames if Jesus leads me, I will pursue it."

That seems to me to be the right spirit, but where do you find it nowadays? The modern spirit mutters, "We are all right, every one of us." He who says "yes" is right, and he who says "no" is also right. You hear a man talk with mawkish sentimentality which he calls Christian charity. "Well, I am of opinion that if a man is a Mahometan or a Catholic or a Mormonite or a dissenter, if he is sincere, he is all right." They do not quite include Devil worshipers, thugs, and cannibals yet, but if things go on, they will accept them into the happy family of the Broad Church. Such is the talk and cant of this present age, but I bear my witness that there is no truth in it, and I call upon every child of God to protest against it and, like Moses, to declare that he can have no complicity with such a confederacy. There is truth somewhere, let us find it; the lie is not of the truth, let us abhor it. There is a God, let us follow Him, and it cannot be that false gods are gods too. Surely truth is of some value to the sons of men; surely there must be something worth holding, something worth contending for, and something worth dying for; but it does not appear nowadays as if men thought so. May we have a respect for God's true church in the world which abides by the apostolic word and doctrine. Let us find it out and join with it and at its side fight for God and for His truth!

Once again, Moses had faith in the "recompense of the reward." He said thus within himself, "I must renounce much and reckon to lose rank, position, and treasure; but I expect to be a gainer notwithstanding, for there will be a day when God shall judge the sons of men. I expect a judgment throne with its impartial balances, and I expect that those who serve God faithfully shall then turn out to have been the wise men and the right men, while those who truckled and bowed down to gain a present ease shall find that they missed eternity while they were snatching after time and that they bartered heaven for a paltry mess of pottage." With this upon his mind, you could not persuade Moses that he ought to compromise and must not be uncharitable and ought not to judge other good people but should be large minded and remember Pharaoh's daughter and how kindly she had nurtured him and consider what opportunities he had of doing good where he was. How he might befriend his poor brethren, what influence he might have over Pharaoh, how he might be the means of leading the princes and the people of Egypt in the right way, and perhaps God had raised him up on purpose to be there who could tell, and so-on, and so-on, and so-on—you know the Babylonian talk, for in these days you have all read or heard the plausible arguments of the deceivableness of unrighteousness, which in these last days teaches men to do evil that good may come. Moses cared for none of these things. He knew his duty and did it, whatever might be the consequences. Every Christian man's duty is to believe the truth and follow the truth and leave results with God. Who dares do that? He is a king's son. But again I say it, who dares do that in these days?

The Arguments Which Supported
Moses' Decision of Following God

The first argument would be, he saw clearly that God was God and therefore must keep His word, must bring His people up out of Egypt and give them a heritage. Now he said within himself, "I desire to be on the right side. God is almighty, God is all truthful, God is altogether just. I am on God's side, and being on God's side, I will prove my truthfulness by leaving the other side altogether."

Then, secondly, we have it in the text that he perceived the pleasures of sin to be but for a season. He said to himself, "I may have but a short time to live, and even if I live to a good old age, life at the longest is still short. When I come to the close of life, what a miserable reflection it will be that I have had all my pleasure; it is all over, and now I have to appear before God as a traitorous Israelite who threw up his birthright for the sake of enjoying the pleasures of Egypt." Oh that men would measure everything in the scales of eternity! We shall be before the bar of God all of us in a few months or years, and then think you how shall we feel? One will say, "I never thought about religion at all." Another, "I thought about it, but I did not think enough to come to any decision upon it. I went the way the current went." Another will say, "I knew the truth well enough, but I could not bear the shame of it; they would have thought me fanatical if I had gone through with it." Another will say, "I halted between two opinions; I hardly thought I was justi-fied in sacrificing my children's position for the sake of being out-and-out a follower of truth." What wretched reflections will come over men who have sold the Savior as Judas did! What wretched deathbeds must they have who have been unfaithful to their consciences and untrue to their God! But oh! with what composure will the believer look forward to another world! He will say, "By grace I am saved, and I bless God I could afford to be ridiculed; I could bear to be laughed at. I could lose that situation; I could be turned out of that farm and could be called a fool, and yet it did not hurt me. I found solace in the society of Christ; I went to Him about it all, and I found that to be reproached for Christ was a sweeter thing than to possess all the treasures of Egypt. Blessed be His name! I missed the pleasures of the world, but they were no miss to me. I was glad to miss them, for I found sweeter pleasure in the company of my Lord, and now there are pleasures to come which shall never end." O brethren, to be out-and-out for Christ; to go to the end with Him, even though it involve the loss of all things, this will pay in the long run. It may bring upon you much disgrace for the present, but that will soon be over, and then comes the eternal reward.

And, then, again, he thought within himself that even the pleasures which did last for a season, while they lasted, were not equal to the pleasure of being reproached for Christ's sake. This ought also to strengthen us, that the worst of Christ is better than the best of the world, that even now we have more joy as Christians, if we are sincere, than we could possibly derive from the sins of the wicked.

I have only this to say in closing. First, we ought all of us to be ready to part with everything for Christ, and if we are not, we are not His disciples. "Master, thou sayest a hard thing," says one. I say it yet again, for a greater Master has said it—"He that loveth son or daughter more than me is not worthy of me." "Unless a man forsake all that he has he cannot be my disciples." Jesus may not require you actually to leave anything, but you must be ready to leave everything if required.

The second observation is this—we ought to abhor the very thought of obtaining honor in this world by concealing our sentiments or by making compromises. If there is a chance of your being highly esteemed by holding your tongue, speak at once and do not run the risk of winning such dishonorable honor. If there is a hope of people praising you because you are so ready to yield your convictions, pray God to make you like a flint never to yield again; for what more damning glory could a man have than to be applauded for disowning his principles to please his fellowmen! From this may the Lord save us!

The third teaching is that we ought to take our place with those who truly follow God and the Scriptures, even if they are not altogether what we should like them to be. The place for an Israelite is with the Israelites; the place for a Christian man is with Christian men. The place for a thorough going disciple of the Bible and of Christ is with others who are such, and even if they should happen to be the lowest in the land and the poorest of the poor and the most illiterate and uneducated persons of the period, what is all this if their God loves them and if they love God? Weighed in the scales of truth, the least one among them is worth ten thousand of the greatest ungodly men.

Lastly, we must all of us look to our faith. Faith is the main thing. You cannot make a thorough character without sincere faith. Begin there, dear hearer. If you are not a believer in Christ, if you believe not in the one God, may the Lord convert you and give you now that precious gift! To try and raise a character which shall be good without a foundation of faith is to build upon the sand and to pile up wood and hay and stubble, which wood, hay, and stubble are very good things as wood, hay, and stubble, but they will not bear the fire. As every Christian character will have to bear fire, it is well to build on the rock and to build with such graces and fruits as will endure trial. You will have to be tried, and if you have, by sneaking through life as a coward, avoided all opposition and all ridicule, ask yourself whether you really are a disciple of that master of the house whom they called Beelzebub, whether you are truly a follower of that crucified Savior who said, "Except a man take up his cross daily and follow me, he cannot be my disciple." Suspect the smooth places; be afraid of that perpetual peace which Christ declares He came to break. He says, "I came not to send peace on the earth, but a sword." He came to bring fire upon the earth; and "what would I," said He, "if it be already kindled."

> Must I be carried to the skies
>   On flowery beds of ease,
> While others fought to win the prize,
>   And sailed through bloody seas.
>
> Sure I must fight if I would reign,
>   Increase my courage, Lord,
> I'd bear the toil, endure the pain,
>   Supported by thy Word. Amen.

5

The Shining of the Face of Moses

And it came to pass, when Moses came down from mount Sinai with the two tables of testimony in Moses' hand, when he came down from the mount, that Moses wist not that the skin of his face shone while he talked with him. And when Aaron and all the children of Israel saw Moses, behold, the skin of his face shone; and they were afraid to come nigh him. And Moses called unto them; and Aaron and all the rulers of the congregation returned unto him: and Moses talked with them. And afterward all the children of Israel came nigh: and he gave them in commandment all that the Lord had spoken with him in mount Sinai. And till Moses had done speaking with them, he put a vail on his face. But when Moses went in before the Lord to speak with him, he took the vail off, until he came out. And he came out, and spake unto the children of Israel that which he was commanded. And the children of Israel saw the face of Moses, that the skin of Moses' face shone: and Moses put the vail upon his face again, until he went in to speak with him (Exodus 34:29–35).

A fast of forty days does not improve the appearance of a man's countenance: he looks starved, wrinkled, old, haggard. Moses had fasted forty days twice at the least; and according to many competent authorities the tenth chapter of Deuteronomy seems to imply that he fasted forty days three times in quick succession. I will not assert or deny the third forty days; but it is certain that, with a very slight interval, Moses fasted forty days and then forty days more; and it is probable that to these must be added a third forty. Small attractiveness would naturally remain in a face which had endured so stern an ordeal;

This sermon was taken from *The Metropolitan Tabernacle Pulpit* and was preached on Sunday morning, May 4, 1890.

but the Lord whom he served made his face brilliant with an unusual luster. The glory of the light of God upon his countenance may have been the reason why he remained so hale in his later years of old age. This man of eighty spent forty years more in guiding Israel, and in the end his eye had not dimmed, nor his natural force abated. He that could fast forty days would be a hard morsel for death. Those eyes which had looked upon the glory of God were not likely to wax dim amid earthly scenes; and that natural force which had endured the vision of the supernatural could well support the fatigues of the wilderness. God so sustained his servant that his long and repeated fasting, during which he did not even drink water, did no harm to his physical constitution. The abstinence even from water renders the fast the more remarkable and lifts it out of similarity to modern feats of fasting.

Moses did not know at the time that his face was shining; but he did know it afterward, and he has here recorded it. He gives in detail the fact of the brightness of his own face, and how others were struck with it, and what he had to do in order to associate with them. We are sure that this record was not made by reason of vanity, for Moses writes about himself in great lowliness of spirit. It was written under divine direction with a worthy object. The man Moses was very meek, and his meekness entered into his authorship, as into all the other acts of his life. We are therefore sure that this record is for our profit. I am afraid, brethren, that God could not afford to make our faces shine. We should grow too proud. It needs a very meek and lowly spirit to bear the shinings of God. We only read of two men whose faces shone, and both were very meek. The one is Moses in the Old Testament; the other is Stephen in the New, whose last words proved his meekness. For, when the Jews were stoning him, he prayed, "Lord, lay not this sin to their charge." Gentleness of nature and lowliness of mind are a fine background on which God may lay the brightness of His glory. Where these things abound, it may be safe for the Lord not only to put His beauty upon a man but also to make a record of the fact. Moses wrote this record with a reluctant pen. Since he did not write it out of vanity, let us not read it out of curiosity. He wrote it for our learning. Let us learn by it; and may God the Holy Spirit cause our faces to shine today, as we read of the shining face of Moses!

It would appear, so far as we can make out the narrative, that his face continued to shine long afterward. After Moses had come down from the mount, the brightness began to diminish. Paul tells us that it was a "glory to be done away"; but when he went into the holy place to commune with God, the brightness was revived, and he came out again and spoke to the people with that same glowing heaven upon his brow. When he addressed the people in the name of God, he took off the veil and let them see the brightness of God in his ambassador; but as soon as he had done speaking and fell back into his own private character, he drew a veil over his face that none might be kept at a distance thereby. The man Moses was as meek with the glory on his countenance as before it gathered there. God put great honor upon him, but he did not desire to make a display of that honor nor childishly wish that it should be seen of men. For the people's sakes and for typical purposes, he veiled his face while in ordinary conversation with the people and only unveiled it when he spoke in the name of the Lord. Brethren, if God honors you as preachers or teachers, accept the honor, but do not attribute it to your own worthiness or even to your own personality; but ascribe it to the office to which the Lord has called you. "I magnify mine office," said Paul; but you never find Paul magnifying himself. He wears the glory as an ambassador of God, not as a private individual. The dignity that God gives to His servants is bestowed upon their office, not upon themselves apart from it. They must never run away with it into daily life and think that they themselves are "reverend" because their Lord is so; nor may they claim for their own thoughts the serious attention which they rightly demand for the Word of the Lord. Ministers, do not pretend to be a class of sacred beings like the Brahmins of India. The only vantage-ground they occupy is that the Lord speaks through them according to the gift of His Holy Spirit. Unveiled are our faces when we speak to God and for God; but among our brethren we would hide away anything from which we might claim superiority for ourselves.

How Did This Glory Come to Be on Moses' Face?

With this as my preface, I shall now come immediately to my subject. Here is Moses with a strange glory upon his countenance. The skin of Moses' face shone; how came it to do so?

The answer is, first, *it was a reflection of the glory which he had seen when he was with God in the holy mount*. It was the result of that partly answered prayer, "I beseech thee, show me thy glory." God could not, at that time, grant the prayer in its fullness, for Moses was not capable of the vision; and the Lord told him, "Thou canst not see my face, and live." I look upon that prayer, however, as a very wonderful one for this reason, that it was answered to the full, fourteen hundred years after it was presented. The glory of God is only to be seen in the face of Christ Jesus; and on the top of Tabor, Moses saw the Son of God transfigured, and his prayer was there and then answered to its utmost bounds. In the transfiguration, God showed to Moses His full glory, for he was then made able to behold it. But though on the top of mount Sinai, he could not see the full glory of Jehovah, yet he had seen enough to make an impression upon him of such a kind that the skin of his face shone. God is light, and they that look upon Him are enlightened and reflect light around them. Moses spoke with God face-to-face as a man speaks with his friend, and this made his countenance glow. As the sun shining upon a reflector has its light thrown back again, often in a most brilliant fashion so that the reflector looks like a minor sun, so was it with the face of Moses when it reflected the glory of the Lord. The face of Moses was to God what the moon is to the sun. A saintly light shines on men when God has shone on him. We are changed into the same image, from glory to glory, as by the presence of the Lord. Would you shine in the valley? First go up the mount and commune with God. Would you shine, my brethren, with superior radiance? Then be this your fervent prayer, "Make thy face to shine upon thy servant." If the Lord lift upon you the light of *His* countenance, there will be no lack of light in *your* countenance. In God's light you shall give light.

The light on the face of Moses was *the result of fellowship with God.* That fellowship was of no common order. It was special and distinguished. I do not doubt that Moses walked with God after the fashion of believing men in the pursuit of his daily calling; but he spent two periods of forty days each in solitary fellowship with God. Everybody was away; Aaron, Joshua, and all the rest were far down below, and Moses was alone with God. His relationship with God was intense, close, and familiar, and that not for one day but for eighty days at the least. Protracted fellowship brings a nearness which brief communion cannot attain. Each morning's sun found him still in the light of God; each evening's dew found his soul still saturated with the divine influence. What must be the effect of such wholehearted, undisturbed fellowship with God? He heard no hum of the camp below; not even the lowing of cattle or bleating of sheep came up from the foot of the mount. Moses had forgotten the world, save only as he pleaded for the people in an agony of prayer. No interests, either personal or family, disturbed his communion; he was oblivious of everything but Jehovah, the Glorious One, who completely overshadowed him. Oh, for the enjoyment of such heavenly communion! My brothers and sisters, have we not lost a great deal by so seldom dwelling apart, so little seeking continuous, absorbing fellowship with the Most High? I am sure we have. We snatch a hasty minute of prayer; we afford a hurried quarter of an hour for Bible reading, and we think we have done well. Very far am I from saying that it is not well. But if for minutes we had hours, the gain might increase in proportion. Oh, for nights of prayer! Oh, for the close shutting of the closet door, and a believer drawing nigh to God! There is no limit to the power we might obtain if such were the case. Though our faces might not be lit up with splendor, our lives would shine, our characters would become more pure and transparent; and our whole spirit would be so heavenly that men would regard with wonder the brightness of our being. Thus, you see, the face of Moses shone because he had long looked upon the face of God.

I would have you note that this communion with God *included intense intercession for the people*. God will not have fellowship with our selfishness. Moses came out of himself and became an intense pleader for the people; and thus he became like the Son of God, and the glory descended on him. How he pleaded! With what sighs and cries he besought Jehovah not to destroy the men who had vexed His Holy Spirit! They had degraded the Godhead by likening it to a bullock which eats grass. They made a calf in Horeb and bowed before it, saying, "These be thy gods, O Israel"! Moses pleaded for the people down below and not for himself. Here is a point in which, it may be, we fail. The Lord turned again the captivity of Job when he prayed for his friends. The Lord loves intercessory prayer; and if ever He makes a man's face to shine, it is when he, like Christ, has made intercession for the transgressors and poured out his soul, not for himself, but for a guilty company.

More than that. In that intercession Moses had exhibited a degree of self-abnegation reaching to the sublime. God said to him, "Let me alone, that I may destroy them. I will make of thee a great nation." The Lord's covenant with Abraham was that Abraham's seed should possess the land; but the Lord might have destroyed all the existing tribes except Moses and then have made of the family of Moses a race in which the covenant with Abraham could have been kept to the letter. What a prospect was set before him! The children of Moses should grow into an elect nation, heirs of all the promises of God. But no! Moses not only goes the length of putting aside the proffered honor, but he cries, "Blot me, I pray thee, out of thy book which thou hast written." Instead of his name being written in the place of the people, he would let their names stand at the expense of his own. When a man can come to that, he is the man the skin of whose face is a fit parchment on which God may write the glory of His love. The less of self the more of God. When we can renounce all for God's glory and the good of His church, the Lord will not fail to smile upon us.

Yet once more. This man Moses not only obtained this brightness by his long communion and his intercessory prayer and self-oblivion but by *his faithfulness among the people*. When he went down in the interval between the two fastings and found the people worshiping the golden calf, he did not spare them. He loved them, but he did not keep back the stern blow of justice. He said, "Who is on the Lord's side?" And there came to him the tribe of Levi, and he said, "Go through the camp, and slay every man his brother who shall be found rebelling against the Lord." At once they cut off the idolaters who were guilty of open treason against the King of Israel. But this was not enough; the whole nation must be chastened for its great sin and humbled by a symbolical punishment. I think I see Moses, having broken the tables in his holy wrath, now taking down their idol god, grinding it, pounding it, dissolving it in water, and sternly compelling the tribes to drink of the water. He made a nauseous, bitter draught out of their idol and made them drink it, so that their bellies might be filled with their own iniquity and they might know what it was to turn away from the Lord their God. Grand old Moses! Faithful servant of God! Unbending executioner of divine justice! Meek were you, but by no means indifferent to truth and righteousness. God chooses not milksops, destitute of backbone, to wear His glory upon their faces. We have plenty of men made of sugar, nowadays, that melt into the stream of popular opinion; but these shall never ascend into the hill of the Lord nor stand in His holy place nor wear the tokens of His glory. O my brother, it is needful that you be true to the Lord in public if you would have His fellowship in private. If the Lord can challenge you for your unfaithfulness among men, He will never honor you with His own peculiar seal of light. Moses was no trimmer, no hunter after popularity; but he was sternly true to his Lord, and hence he was such that the Lord could safely make his face to shine. Enough of this, though much more might be said; learn the useful lesson which this part of the subject teaches.

What Did This Shining of His Face Mean?

This brightness on his face—what did it signify? Very briefly, it meant this: *God's special favor for Moses*. God seemed to say, "This is my man. I have chosen him above all others. Among those that are born of women there is no greater than he. I have put a measure of My own glory upon him, and the token thereof shines in his face."

Surely, it also meant *special favor for Israel*. If they could but have understood it, they would not have been afraid; but conscience made them cowards. God, in effect, said to them, by the shining of the face of Moses, "I have had favor upon you, for I have accepted your intercessor. My servant Moses has been pleading for your lives, and in proof that I have accepted you and will spare you, I have written your pardon across his shining brow." Favor to the Lord Jesus is favor to us. Lord, when I hear You say, "This is my beloved Son, in whom I am well pleased," I rejoice that You are well pleased with me in Christ Jesus. When God looks on the face of His Anointed, He looks with favor upon us.

This brightness on the face of Moses was also *God's witness to his commission*. He had sent him, for He had glorified him. The people could not doubt his commission when they looked upon his shining face. I suppose rays of light proceeded from it. Michael Angelo, in his famous statue of Moses, represents him with horns. The strange fancy is founded on the Vulgate version, which mistook the meaning of a Hebrew word and translated it "horns." Beams of light seemed to rise from that marvelous face. A halo of glory surrounded that solemn countenance, and the people could not but perceive that this was a man on whom God had looked.

And more. It was not only a witness of his office, but it was *an increase of his power*. The people were overawed by this strange light. They dared, even after this, to murmur against Moses, for they dared to murmur against God Himself; but, still, to a people of such a temper as theirs, the supernatural light must have been a source of wonder and of awe.

> They gazed and looked, and lo, on brow and face,
>   A glory and a brightness not of earth,
> The eye lit up with fire of heavenly birth,
>   The whole man bright with beams of God's great grace.

It gave their prophet authority with them; it made them tremble before him. They would not dare to contradict one who looked on them with such a face of glory. His speech was as a flame of fire, because his face was on a blaze.

The pith of the whole thing, I think, lies in this—*the face of Moses shone typically, to show us that there is a great glory about the law of God*. It has a glory all its own from its spirituality, its holiness, its perfectness, its justice, its immutability, its power over the conscience, and so forth. It has eminent glory, because it has been ordained of God Himself and therefore stands as the sacred rule of the universe. But this is not what Paul understands by the glory of the law. He makes the glory "of that which was to be abolished" the glory of the ceremonial law, to lie in its end. Now, the end of the law for righteousness is Christ. The law is given to point us to Christ, to drive us to Christ, to be our schoolmaster to whip us to Christ, to convince us of our need of Christ, and to shut us out from every other hope but that which begins and ends with Christ. The glory of the law is Christ. And so Moses comes with a glory on his face which the children of Israel could not perceive nor steadfastly look into.

> They looked and saw the glory, and they shrank
> From that dread vision, dazzling man's frail sight.

Even as today men see outward rites that God has given but see not their glorious meaning, so was it with Israel in the wilderness. They saw sacrifices, but they knew not the Great Sacrifice; they saw the oil and the water, but they knew not the Holy Spirit; they saw ten thousand tokens dear and manifest of the ever-blessed Messiah, but they did not perceive Him so as to know Him when He came. Every type and ceremony might say, "Who hath believed our report? and to whom is the arm of the Lord revealed?" The law is overlaid with the glory of Christ, as the face of Moses was covered with light. This is the deepest and innermost meaning of the sacred light which glowed upon the skin of the face of Moses.

This Glory upon the Face of Moses—
Why Did Not Moses Know of It?

I answer, first, that it is not easy for a man to see his own face, unless he can borrow a looking-glass. Speaking in parable, the meaning I intend is this: it is not easy for a man to form an accurate judgment of his own character. There are people in the world who think they see their own faces clearly and that they shine like suns; and yet they do not shine at all, except it be with brazen impudence and self-conceit. In other cases, lowly men are afraid that their faces do not shine at all; and yet they are brightness itself. It is no small part of the shining of some faces that their owners are modest and humble. Brethren, you cannot see your own faces; and until you can do so, you must not imagine that you know your own characters. Upon reflection, you may arrive at something like a judgment, but it is not one which you may safely rely upon. Since Moses had no looking-glass, how could he tell that the skin of his face shone? Our own judgment of our own character usually errs on the side of partiality to ourselves. Nor is the evil so readily cured as some suppose, for the gift of seeing ourselves "as others see us" is not so corrective as might be supposed. Some persist in seeing us through the colored spectacles of prejudice and ill-will, and this injustice is apt to create in us a further partiality to ourselves. If other men make mistakes about us who can see us, they probably do not make such great blunders about us as we do about ourselves, since we cannot see our own faces. Truth to tell, we are very fond of ourselves and have our own characters in high esteem; therefore we are unfair judges on points of difficulty about ourselves. Our temptation is to gross self-flattery. We dream of strength where all is weakness, of wisdom where all is folly. A man does not need to see his own face. If that face be washed to purity, it will be enough that God sees it and approves its beauty.

But I will tell you, further, why Moses did not see the glory of his own face. It was because *he had seen the glory of God.* When a man gets a clear view of the holiness of God, it is all over with all claim of personal excellence; from that day he abhors himself in dust and ashes. I might have thought myself pure; but how can I, when I find that the heavens are not clean in God's sight? I might have thought myself wise; but how can I, when I read that He charged His angels with folly? How can I speak of perfect purity as a thing of which I am possessed, after I have seen the King, the Lord of Hosts? A vision of God is the death of boasting. He that has looked into the face of the sun is blinded to all other light.

Having given one sufficient reason, I am, perhaps, unwise to add another; but yet it may be profitable to remember that Moses had not seen the shining of his own face because *it had never once entered his thoughts to wish that his face should shine.* That is true beauty of character which comes without being sought—I mean unconscious excellence, a character which commands an admiration which it has never desired. Are we not too apt to wish to be bright that others may see us? Have we not labored to grow in grace that we might outgrow others? Does no man pray for success in his ministry with a little squint of his eye toward an ambition to be thought "so useful"? Does no sister ever seek the salvation of her class that she may be esteemed in the church as a remarkable soulwinner? Did you never pray for holiness and really mean that you wished to be considered holy? Have you never prayed in public with great fervor with a half-suppressed wish to be thought a special man of God? Would it not have greatly gratified you to hear men say, "What a prayer that was!"? Have you not even labored to be humble that you might rejoice in your humility? I am afraid it is so. We are always praying, "Lord, make my face to shine," but Moses never had such a wish; and, therefore, when it did shine, he did not know it. He had not laid his plans for such an honor. Let us not set traps for personal reputation or even glance a thought that way.

Another reason why he had not thought of it was that *he was so much engaged in doing good to others.* He gave himself up for those stiff-necked Israelites; he actually lived for them and offered himself before God to die for them. He carried the whole people in his bosom as a nurse carries her child. He fed his flock like a shepherd; and, like the Good Shepherd, he would have given his life for the sheep. Oh, the self-sacrifice of the man Moses! He never thought about his own face, for he was thinking about *their* faces. What would he have given if they had been capable of such nearness to God as he himself enjoyed! Oh, to be so absorbed in doing good that we have not a thought or a care for our own personal repute! Then a man may do good in self-forgetfulness, and may find himself famous to his own amazement.

Once more, Moses could not very well have thought of his own face shining, for *he had no example of such a thing to suggest the idea.* Out of all those around him nobody else's face shone. When you live with men whose faces shine, then you inquire about yourself, for you naturally wish your face to shine like theirs. Aaron's face did not shine.

Alas, poor Aaron! Nobody's face shone in all that camp, and so there was nothing to cause Moses to look for such a radiance on his own brow. Mr. Bunyan, in his beautiful picture of Christiana and Mercy and the children coming up from the bath, represents the opposite state of things, for he says, "When the women were thus adorned, they seemed to be a terror one to the other; for that they could not see that glory each one on herself which they could see in each other. Now, therefore, they began to esteem each other better than themselves. 'For you are fairer than I am,' said one. And 'You are more comely than I am,' said another. The children also stood amazed to see into what fashion they were brought." It is a great treat to see and admire the Christian virtues of our brethren in Christ. Every Christian delights to see his friends comely in all the graces of the Holy Spirit. Moses had but little to gratify him in that way, especially at the period when he came down from the mount and found Aaron weakly yielding to the people's sin. Even the choicest of the elders were far inferior to Moses, and therefore it was not suggested by his surroundings that his own face might shine.

It is well when men are not self-conscious. It is best, my beloved brethren, that our faces should shine to others and not to ourselves. If you might know your own excelling, do not know it, for there is an ill savor about self-consciousness. To come forward and say, "I am perfectly holy," is babyish. It is like a child who cries, "See my new frock! Look at my pretty new frock!" I tremble to hear one say, "I have quite passed out of the conflict mentioned in the seventh of Romans. I have got this, and I have got that." I am reminded of Jehu, when he said, "Come with me, and see my zeal for the Lord"; and yet Jehu was not right at heart before the Lord. There is not much to see when you wish men to see it. God save us from knowing too much about the shining of our own faces! May the light of His countenance fill the whole circle of our being, while we lie at His feet, mastered by a reverent awe of Him!

Why Did Moses Wear a Veil?

I answer, *in part the natural meekness of the man led him to do so.* He was forced into the position of leader; he never wished to be prominent, but the Lord put great pressure upon him in the desert and drove him on to be as king in Jeshurun. He had no ambitions. Though made to be as God to Pharaoh, he never exalted himself in the Egyptian court. Among the Israelites he did not monopolize power, but he gladly yielded to the chosen elders a portion of his magisterial dignity. The man Moses was very meek, and so to hide the brightness of his face was a pleasure and not a trial to him. Like many a lovely woman, he shrank from the public gaze. We shall do well to possess the grace of humility.

He veiled his face *in tender condescension to the people*. When they ran away from him, he called to them to know why they were afraid. "My lord, we fear that splendor on your brow." "Then, let me veil it," says he; "I would not terrify, but win." It was their fault that they could not bear the brightness—their fault—I say again, their *fault*, and yet he does not upbraid nor stand upon his rights. He had compassion on their folly as well as on their weakness. It may happen that a gracious man may be so evidently right, that, when others are offended at him, the offense is to be greatly blamed; and yet he will do well to yield in anything which does not involve principle. There is a modest veiling of excellences which shows a brother to be still more excellent than his excellences which have proved him. Quench not the light of your sternest principle, but veil it with abounding love. He always sinks himself, this man Moses. The God-given glory of *his* face he does not slight nor seek to abate; but so far as it would bring him honor from men, he puts it under a veil. That he may come closer to the people whom he loves, he is content to hide his glory. Let us also seek to bless the people and to keep in touch with them.

But, beloved, the chief reason lies elsewhere. Why did Moses veil his face? The answer is this: *it was a judicial symbol, setting forth the sentence of God upon the people.* The Lord, by this token, as good as said, "You are so rebellious, so given to your idolatries, so unwilling to see, that henceforth you shall not see the brightness of my glory in the dispensation of the law in which you live. Moses shall veil his face because the veil is upon your hearts." It is a dreadful thing when God gives men up to a judicial blindness, when he permits the veil which they have woven to abide over their minds, "that seeing they might not see; and hearing they might not understand." As I told you in the reading, the veil was literally on Moses' face, but spiritually it was on their hearts. Henceforth they were not to see because they had not wished to see. He that willfully shuts his eyes will find that God takes away his sight. If you refuse to understand, justice will make you foolish. The shadow of destruction is insensibility. The eyes are blindfolded before the fatal volley is fired.

The practical warning I would earnestly apply. Do you not think we have a great many people around us—may we not belong to them ourselves?—whose foolish hearts are blinded so that the light of the glory of God in the face of Christ is veiled for them? Are not many suffering from veiled hearts? In your circle there is a rare man of God. You have heard of his faith. He walks with God. Others have told you what beauties they see in his character. You cannot see anything particular in him; you, on the contrary, despise him and avoid his company. He wears a veil for you. Here is the Bible. "O book, exquisite sweetness!" Your dear mother calls it beyond all things precious. Dear soul, how her face brightens when she tells you how she has been sustained by it in the day of trouble! You read it now and then, but you do not see anything remarkable in it, certainly nothing that charms you—the Book is veiled to you. Here is the glorious Gospel of the blessed God. You have heard us say what a wonderful Gospel it is. We have been overjoyed in describing it. You feel no enthusiasm. The Gospel is veiled to you. You have heard a sermon on some grand doctrine. Believers are ready to leap for joy, but you are utterly indifferent. The truth is veiled to you. This is a sad omen of a lost estate. The veil is on your heart, and your soul is in darkness which may be felt. Am I not speaking the truth about many of you? O my friends, when you hear about Christ and do not admire Him, conclude that you must be blinded; when you hear the glorious Gospel of the blessed God and it does not charm you, conclude that the veil is on your hearts. Oh, that you would turn to the Lord! For when you turn to God, the veil shall be taken away. Oh, that God the Holy Spirit would come and turn you by His almighty power! May He constrain you to seek the Lord today. Then shall the veil be taken away, and you shall see the beauty of the Lord Jesus in His salvation. Here is a little prayer for you—use it often—"Open thou mine eyes, that I may behold wondrous things out of thy law." The wondrous things are in the law; may you behold them. The Holy Spirit must take the veil away and remove the scales from your eyes, and then you will see, but not until then.

This is why Moses wore the veil—as a testimony that God had given them over to judicial blindness, because they refused to know His will. O Lord, deal not thus with this people!

What Other Lessons May We Learn from the Face of Moses?

First, learn *the exceeding glory of our Lord Jesus Christ.* How so? Well, this was, so to speak in a minor degree, the transfiguration of Moses; and all it came to was that his face shone. But when Christ came, He was transfigured as to His whole person. Not only His face shone, but His whole person and His garments also. Moses could veil his face, but the shining of our Lord could not be thus veiled, for it streamed through His raiment which became "white and glistering." The veil of Moses was, so to speak, a raiment for his face, and it was able to keep in the glory; but our Lord was wearing His usual garment without seam, woven from the top throughout, and the light shone through His raiment so that He and His clothing were alike bright. Nothing could conceal the glory of our Lord which was so great that, whereas Israel saw it tremblingly, the disciples were cast into a deep sleep thereby. A word is used by an instructive commentator in reference to Christ's transfiguration which expresses a forcible idea: he speaks of it as incandescence. He was all brightness and light, surpassing the mere shining of the skin even as the sun far surpasses every form of its reflection. The glory of Christ is beyond all comparison—the glory which excels. Oh, that I knew how to speak of it! But I feel like Paul, when he said, "I could not see for the glow of that light." It overpowers me. The Lamb is the light of heaven itself; what shall I say more? John on the rock of Patmos saw our Lord in vision, and he said His "countenance was as the sun shineth in his strength. And when I saw him I fell at his feet as dead." Moses wore a light on his face that might be covered; but Jesus was, and is, all light, and in Him is no darkness at all. "That was the true light, which lighteth every man that cometh into the world." "The law was given by Moses, but grace and truth came by Jesus Christ."

Another lesson is just this. *See the possibilities of glory which await human nature.* If Moses' face can shine here, I can understand how in the next state, when we are risen from the dead, our bodies may be all light and bright and we ourselves like flames of fire. "This corruptible must put on incorruption, and this mortal must put on immortality." Unless our Well-beloved comes quickly, our bodies will be sown in dishonor; and now I see how they can be raised in glory. Then shall we put on "the glory of the celestial." We shall be among the shining ones and shall ourselves shine forth as the sun in the kingdom of our Father. If the wrinkled face of the patriarch Moses, bronzed and browned by forty years in the Arabian desert and lined by the long fast on the top of the mountain—if the dry parchment of his face could shine so marvelously, why should not our bodies be endowed with glory when God shall raise them again from the grave? As a crocus bulb looks up from the soil wherein it was buried and boldly lifts up a golden cup which the sun fills with glory from the heavens, why should not we also bloom into perfection? "Beloved, now are we the sons of God, and it doth not yet appear what we shall be"—any more than it did appear what Moses should be—"but we know that, when he shall appear"—whose appearing is more glorious than that of Moses—"we shall be like him; for we shall see him as he is."

Lastly, here is one more lesson. *What honor God may put upon any one of us if we really put honor upon Him!* My brothers, my sisters, if you are consecrated to God as Moses was, He can give you an unconscious influence which others will be compelled to recognize. Upon your brow the heavenly light of grace will rest; from your eyes the lamp of truth will shine. Walk in the light, as God is in the light, and have fellowship with Him; and then you, too, shall shine as God's light-bearers, and your whole life shall be as the star which guided the wise men to Christ. Influencing men for God, the gracious will follow you, and the wicked will be awed by you, even as "Herod feared John, knowing that he was a just man and holy."

O Spirit of God, rest on every one of us according to our capacity to endure the tongue of fire! Say to us, O Savior, this morning, "Go forth, my friends, and be burning and shining lights to My praise." Amen.

6

David: The Lion-Slayer— The Giant-Killer

Thy servant slew both the lion and the bear and this uncircumcised Philistine shall be as one of them, seeing he hath defied the armies of the living God. David said moreover, the Lord that delivered me out of the paw of the lion and out of the paw of the boar, he will deliver me out of the hand of this Philistine (1 Samuel 17:36–37).

We have all thought a great deal of the courage of David in meeting giant Goliath, but probably we have not given him credit for his conduct in a previous contest. We have not sufficiently noticed that immediately before the encounter with the Philistine he fought a battle which cost him far more thought, prudence, and patience. The word-battle in which he had to engage with his brothers and with king Saul was a more trying ordeal to him than going forth in the strength of the Lord to smite the uncircumcised boaster. Many a man meets with more trouble from his friends than from his enemies; and when he has learned to overcome the depressing influence of prudent friends, he makes short work of the opposition of avowed adversaries.

Observe that David had first to contend with his own brothers. I hardly think Eliab was so much swayed by envy as has been supposed. I fancy that Eliab had too much contempt for his young brother to envy him; he thought it ridiculous that a youth so given to music and piety and gentle pursuits should dream of encountering a giant. He derided the idea of his being equal to such a task and only feared lest in a moment of foolish enthusiasm he might throw his life away in the mad enterprise; and therefore Eliab somewhat superciliously, but still

This sermon was taken from *The Metropolitan Tabernacle Pulpit* and was preached on Sunday morning, September 6, 1875.

somewhat in the spirit natural to an elder brother who feels himself a sort of guardian to the younger members of the house, chided him and told him that only pride and curiosity had brought him there at all and that he had better have remained with his sheep in the wilderness. Such a youth he thought was fitter among lambs than among warriors and more likely to be in his place beneath a tree with his shepherd's pipe than in the midst of a battle. David met this charge in the very wisest way: he answered with a few soft words and then turned away. He did not continue to argue, for in such a contest to multiply words is to increase ill feeling, and he who is first silent is the conqueror. Grandly did this young man restrain himself, though the provocation was very severe, and herein he won the honors of the man who restrains his spirit, and He is greater than the soldier who takes a city. I admire David as he selects his five smooth stones from the brook, but I admire him quite as much when he so gently replies where others might have been angry and then so wisely turns aside from a debate which could not have been to the profit of either party.

Next, he is brought before Saul, and David enters upon a contest with a king to whom he felt loyal respect and with a soldier who had been a man of war from his youth up and had wrought many famous deeds; one, therefore, to whom David looked up with not a little reverence. When king Saul said to him, "Thou art not able to fight with this Philistine, for thou art but a youth and he a man of war from his youth," it must have been somewhat difficult for the young hero to cope with the weighty judgment; and yet he did so, answering meekly, forcibly, and in all respects well. Did you notice how David said to Saul, "Let no man's heart fail because of him." He did not say, "Let not thy heart fail thee"; he was too much of a courtier for that; he had too much delicacy of mind to insinuate that a royal heart could fear. When he proceeded to argue with the king, it was in the most polite and deferential manner. He begins, "Thy servant kept his father's sheep"; he calls himself a servant of the king and does not hesitate to own that he is only a shepherd who had no flock of his own but served under his father. There was nothing like assumption, but the very reverse. Yet while he used soft words, he brought forth hard arguments; he mentioned facts, and these are always the best weapons against carnal reasoning. Saul said, "Thou art not able to meet this Philistine"; but David replied, "Thy servant slew both the lion and the bear." He placed facts against mere opinions and won the day. He did not quote Scripture to the king, for I suppose he knew Saul too well for that and felt that he had not grace enough to be swayed by the promises and examples of Holy Writ. But he brought facts before him, knowing well how to give a reason for the hope that was in him with meekness and fear. His arguments quite overcame the opposition of Saul, which would have damped the enthusiasm of many, and Saul not only commissioned him to go and fight the Philistine, saying, "Go, and the Lord be with thee"; but he actually clothed him in his royal armor, which was of no small value and which of course would have increased the honors of the Philistine champion had David fallen before him. Some little faith in David was kindled in Saul's bosom, and he was willing to trust his armor in his hands. Thus it is clear that David fought the battle with Saul as admirably as he afterward conducted his duel with the giant, and he deserves no small honor for it. No, rather to God be honor who, while He taught His servant's hands to war and his fingers to fight, also taught his tongue to utter right words by which he put to silence those who would have abashed him.

What was the pith of David's argument? What were the five smooth stones which he threw at the head of carnal reasoning? That shall be the subject of this morning's discourse. We will consider the way in which David argued down all doubts and fears and by the Spirit of God was nerved to go forth to deeds of sacred daring in the name of the Most High, for the same conquering arguments may, perhaps, serve our turn also.

Three things are before us in the text, *recollections*, *reasonings*, and *results*.

Recollections

Thy servant kept his father's sheep, and there came a lion, and a bear, and took a lamb out of the flock: and I went out after him, and smote him, and delivered it out of his mouth: and when he arose against me, I caught him by his beard, and smote him, and slew him. Thy servant slew both the lion and the bear. These were noteworthy facts which David had stored up in his memory, and he now mentions them, for they exactly answered his purpose. We ought not to be unmindful of the way by which the Lord our God has led us, for if we are we shall lose much. Some saints have very short memories. It has been well said that we write our benefits in dust and our injuries in marble, and it is equally true that we generally inscribe our afflictions upon brass, while the records of the deliverances of God are written in water. It ought not so to be. If our memories were more tenacious of the merciful visitations of our God, our faith would often be strengthened in times of trial. Now, what did David recollect? I want you to remember the same.

He recollected, first, that, whatever his present trial might be, *he had been tried before*, tried when he was but a young man, peacefully employed in keeping his flocks. A lion rushed upon his prey, and he had to defend his sheep—no small trial for a young man to have to meet a savage beast, strong, furious, and probably ravenous with hunger. Yet the ordeal had not destroyed him, and he felt sure that another of the same kind would not do so. He had encountered that danger in the course of his duty, when he was in his proper place, and engaged in his lawful calling. He had thereby learned that the path of duty is not without its difficulties and perils. He was keeping his flock as he ought to be, and yet a lion attacked him; and so you and I have met with trials which did not arise from sin but, on the other hand, came to us because we conscientiously did the right and would not yield to temptation. We must not think that we are out of the right road when we meet with difficulties, for we must expect through much tribulation to inherit the kingdom of God. Severe afflictions and afflictions arising out of holy walking are not new things to us; let us now remember our old encounters.

He remembered, too, that *he had been tried frequently*. He had been not only attacked by a lion, but also by a bear. He had been tried in different ways, for lions and bears do not fight exactly in the same manner, neither are they to be met with precisely the same tactics. David remembered that his trials had been of different sorts, and that in each case the battle had been hard. It was no small matter to fight hand to hand with a lion, and no child's play to rush single-handed upon a bear. We, also, in looking back, remember sharp encounters with foes of many kinds which were terrible battles to us at the time. Brethren, some of us who have been for years in the ways of the Lord can tell of shrewd brushes with the enemy, and we can speak of wounds and ugly rents of which we wear the seals to this day. Many have been our adversaries and furious, yet have we been upheld until now by Jesus, the Captain of our salvation. Wherefore, then, should we fear concerning the present fiery trial, as though some strange thing had happened to us. Is it a Philistine this time? Well, it was a lion before, and a bear on another occasion. It is only a little change of the same constant trial of our faith, and therefore let us not shrink from the conflict.

Next, David recollected that *he had risked all in the persecution of his duty*. He was set to take care of the sheep and the lambs, and he did so. A lion had dared to leap into the fold and seize a lamb, and without a single thought of anything but the lamb and his own duty, the young shepherd rushed upon the monster with all the ardor of youth and, smiting him with his crook, compelled him to drop his prey. He had put his own life in jeopardy for the poor defenseless lamb. Can you not recollect, my Christian brethren, when you also took no thought as to what you should lose if you followed Christ and cared not if it cost you your very life? With earnest honesty you desired to learn what you ought to do, and you did it, careless of the cost. Reproach, slander, misrepresentation, and unkindness you defied, so long as you could but clear your conscience and honor your Lord. O blessed recklessness! Do you remember those early days when you could cheerfully have gone to prison and to death for Christ's sake? For scriptural doctrines and ordinances you would willingly have suffered martyrdom. Perhaps some of you have on more than one occasion actually risked everything for the sake of integrity and for the honor of the Lord Jesus Christ, even as others have defied the utmost power of Satan and the most virulent hatred of men for the sake of the Lord God of Hosts. You have felt that you could sooner die than deny the truth and sooner perish from off the face of the earth than be craven to the trust which the Lord had committed to you. Look back upon your brave days, my brethren, not that you may be proud of what you did but that you may be ashamed if you are afraid to do the like again. Blush if what you could do as a stripling should appear too hard for you in riper years. These recollections have precious uses; they will lead us to bless God and humble ourselves in His presence.

Next he remembered that *he had on that occasion gone alone to the fray.* The antagonist was a lion, and a dozen men might have found themselves too few for the fight; but David remembered that in that contest he was quite alone. He had not called in the under shepherds to the rescue, but armed only with his crook, he had belabored the lion until the monster found it convenient to leave his prey and turn upon the young shepherd. David was ready for him, seized him by his beard, dashed his head upon the rocks, and did not relinquish his grasp until the king of beasts lay dead at his feet. It was a grand incident, even had it stood alone, but a bear had supplied an equally memorable trophy. Some of us may well recall hours in our past lives when we were all alone, and, as we went forth to serve the Lord Jesus, our enterprise was regarded as Utopian and spoken of as sure to end in failure. Many a good man has gone forth for Christ's sake even worse than alone, for those who should have aided have done their best to criticize and prophesy disaster; but men whom God ordains to honor have shut their ears to critics and pushed on until they have reached success, and then everybody has said, "We always thought so," and not a few have even claimed to have been ardent admirers all along. Brother, do you remember when everyone said you were foolhardy and self-sufficient, and regarded your course as absurd and sure to come to an end? Six months were to see the end of your career, which was a mere bubble and would soon collapse? Ah, those were brave times when the Lord was with you and man's opinion weighed but lightly. It may be that for truth's sake your relatives turned their backs upon you, and no man would say you a good word, and yet in the name of the Lord God of Hosts you did the right and dared all results, and you have had no cause to regret it, but overflowing reasons to bless God that He strengthened you to "dare to be a Daniel and dare to stand alone." Look back at that courageous hour, and now that you are surrounded by a goodly company of friends, think whether you have as simple a trust in God now as you manifested then. If you judge that you have, prove by your actions that you can still dare to go forward under difficulties, unshackled by dependence on an arm of flesh. The discipline of desertion ought not to have been lost upon you; you ought to be all the stronger for having been compelled to walk alone. The friendship of your fellows has been a loss rather than a gain if you cannot now wage single-handed battle as you did in former times. Are you now become slavishly dependent on an arm of flesh? If so, chide yourself by the memories of braver days.

David also recollected that on that occasion when he smote the lion and the bear *he had nothing visible to rely upon, but simply trusted his God.* He had in his hand no sharp weapon of iron with which to smite the wild beast to the heart, but careless as to weapons, he thought only of his God and rushed on the foe. He was as yet a young man; his muscles were not set and strong, neither did he seem fit for such a venturous deed; but his God was almighty, and, reliant upon the omnipotence of God, he thought nothing of his youth but flung himself into the fray. What more in the way of help did he need, since God was with him? Oh, brethren, there were times with some of us when we commenced our work, when our sole reliance was the unseen Lord. We were cast upon the invisible power of God, and if that could fail us, we must go. Our attempts were such as carnal reason could not justify, such indeed as only divine interposition could carry through. They were right enough if the divine power could be calculated on, but apart from that they were well nigh insane. Glory be to God, He has been as good as His word; our faith has been justified by results, and unbelief has been struck dumb. The Lord taught us to rest in Him from our youth up and to declare His wondrous works, and now that we have tried and proved His faithfulness, we dare not hide these things from the generation following. Our witness must be borne even though we should be charged with boasting. "My soul shall make her boast in the Lord." But can it be true that now we have begun coolly to calculate means and to rely upon methods and plans, whereas once we looked to God alone? Do we now trust in this friend and rely on that and distrust the Lord if friends are few? Shame upon us if we do so, for this is to leave the way of victory for the path of defeat, to come down from the heroic track to the common highway of carnal reasoning, and so to fall into care, fretfulness, weakness, and dishonor. Happy is the man who trusts in the Lord alone by unstaggering faith; he shall go from strength to strength, but he who chooses to walk by sight shall utterly decay.

David recollected also that *the tactics which he adopted on that occasion were natural, artless, and vigorous.* All that he did was just to smite the lion and the bear with his staff, or whatever came first to hand, and then to fight as nature and the occasion suggested. He did what his courage prompted, without waiting to consult a committee of lion slayers and bear trappers. His whole art was faith; this was his science and his skill. He consulted not with flesh and blood, followed no precedents, imitated no noted hunters, and encumbered himself with no rules, but he did his best as his faith in God directed him. He threw his whole soul into the conflict and fought vigorously, for his faith did not make him sit still and expect the lion to die in a fit or the bear to become insensible. He seemed to say to himself, "Now, David, if anything is to be done, you must be all here, and every muscle you have must be put to the strain. You have a lion to fight with; therefore stir up your strength, and while you rely upon God alone, take care to play the man this day for your father's flock." Courage supplied coolness; and energy, backed up by confidence, won the day. Do you remember, my brother, when in your own way you did the same? You were reliant upon God but not idle; you put your whole force of soul and energy into your Master's service, as if it all rested on you, and yet you depended wholly on Him and you succeeded! How is it with you now? Do you now take things easily? Do you wonder that you do not succeed? If you are growing cold and careless, if you are getting sleepy and dull, rebuke your soul, and use your past experience as a whip wherewith to flog yourself into energy. Let it never be said that he who woke himself up to fight a lion now falls asleep in the presence of a Philistine.

David remembered *that by confidence in God his energetic fighting gained the victory*—the lion was killed, and the bear was killed too. And cannot you remember, brethren, what victories God gave you? When you were little in Israel and despised, yet His hand was upon you, and when few would bid you God speed, yet the Jehovah of Hosts encouraged your heart, and when you were feeble and but a youth, the Lord Jesus helped you to do exploits for Him in your own way. Remember this, and be of good courage this morning in the conflict which now lies before you. David talked of his former deeds somewhat reluctantly. I do not know that he had ever spoken of them before, and he did so on this occasion with the sole motive of glorifying God, and that he might be allowed to repeat them. He wished for permission from Saul to confront the Philistine champion and bring yet greater glory to God. Brethren, whenever you talk of what God enabled you to do and you lay the stress upon God's enablings and not upon your own doings, and when you rehearse the story of your early days, let it not be as a reason why you should now be exonerated from service and be allowed to retire upon your laurels, but as an argument why you should now be allowed the most arduous and dangerous post in the battle. Let the past be a stepping-stone to something higher, an incentive to nobler enterprise. On, on you soldiers of the Cross, in God's name eclipse your former selves. As grace enabled you to pile the carcass of the bear upon the corpse of the lion, so now resolve that the Philistine shall increase the heap, and his head shall crown the whole, to the honor and glory of the God of Israel. So much for recollections. I pity the man who has none of them, and I pity yet more the man who having them is now afraid to risk all for his Lord.

Reasonings

David used an argument in which no flaw can be found. He said, "The case of this Philistine is a parallel one to that of the lion. If I act in the same manner by faith in God with this giant as I did with the lion, God is the same, and therefore the result will be the same." That seems to me to be very clear reasoning, and I bid you adopt it. Such and such was my past difficulty, and my present trouble is of the same order. In that past trial I rested upon God and acted in a right way, and He delivered me; therefore, if I trust in God still and do as before, He is the same as ever, and I shall triumph yet again.

Let us now consider the case, and we shall see that it really was parallel. There was the flock, defenseless; here was Israel, God's flock, defenseless too, with no one to take up its cause. In all the camp there was not one single man who dared take up the foeman's challenge. David was a shepherd and, therefore, as a shepherd, bound to defend his flock; and in the present instance he remembered, I doubt not, that Samuel had anointed him to be king over Israel, and he felt that some of the responsibility of the anointing rested upon him even then, and that if no man else would play the shepherd, the anointed son of Jesse must do it, and so it looked to him like a parallel case—Israel the flock, and he the shepherd who must defend it.

He was alone that day when he smote the lion, and so he was this day when he was to confront his enormous foe. Of course it was one of the conditions of a duel that the Israelitish champion should go forth alone, and, besides that, there was no one in all the camp who was likely to wish to accompany him upon such an errand. So, now that he was all alone, the case was the more truly parallel.

As for that Philistine, he felt that in him he had an antagonist of the old sort. It was brute force before; it was brute force now. It might take the shape of a lion or a bear or a Philistine, but David considered that it was only so much flesh and bone and muscle, so much brag or roar, tooth or spear. He considered the Philistine to be only a wild animal of another shape, because he was not in covenant with God and dared to put himself in opposition to the Most High. My brethren, a man who has God for a friend is higher than an angel, but a man who is God's enemy is no better than a beast; reckon him so and your fears of him will vanish. Goliath was mighty, but so was the lion; he was cunning of fence, but so was the bear. The case was only a repetition of the former combat. And as God was not with the lion nor with the bear, so David felt that God was not with Goliath and could not be, for he was the enemy of God's Israel; and as God had been with him when fighting the wild beasts, so he felt that God was with him now. It looked to him as if he had already twice gone through a rehearsal of all this when he was in the wilderness alone, and therefore he could the more easily go through it now. Perhaps there flashed on his mind the case of Samson, who learned to slay the Philistines by rending a lion when he was alone in the vineyard. So David felt, "I have killed my lion like Samson, and now like Samson I go to fight this Philistine, or a thousand like him, if need be, in the name of the Lord of Hosts."

The whole argument is this, in the one case by such tactics we have been successful, trusting in God, and therefore in a similar case we have only to do the same, and we shall realize the same victory. Brethren and sisters, here is a fault with most of us, that when we look back upon past deliverances we do not draw this parallel, but on the contrary the temptation haunts us, to think that our present trial is clearly a new case. For instance, David might have said, "When I slew that lion I was younger than I am now, and I had more courage and vivacity, but those shrewd brushes have strained me somewhat, and I had better be more prudent." Just as you and I say sometimes, "Ah, what I did was done when I was a young man, I cannot do the like now. That trouble which I bore so patiently, by God's grace, was in other times, but this affliction has come upon me when I am less able to endure it, for I have not the elasticity of spirit which once I had, nor the vigor I formerly possessed." When we want to escape from some arduous work, we do it by trying to show that we are not under the same obligations as in former days. We know in our conscience that if we did great things when we were young, we ought to do greater things now that we are older, wiser, more experienced, and more trained in war, but we try to argue our conscience into silence. If the Lord helped us to bear with patience or to labor with zeal after all the experience we have had, that patience and zeal should now be easier to us than before. Alas, we do not argue so, but to our shame we excuse ourselves and live ingloriously.

I know a man who today says, "Yes, what we did in years gone by we did in our heroic age, but we are not so enthusiastic now." And why not? We are so apt to magnify our former selves and think of our early deeds as of something to be wondered at but not to be attempted now.

Fools that we are! They were little enough in all conscience and ought to be outdone. Oh, dear brethren, this resting on our oars will not do; we are drifting down with the tide. David did not say, "I slew a lion and a bear, I have had my turn at such boats, let somebody else go and fight that Philistine." Yet we have heard people say, "When I was a young man, I taught in the Sunday school; I used to go out preaching in the villages, and so on." Oh, brother, and why not do it now? I think you ought to be doing more instead of less. As God gives you more knowledge, more experience, and more grace, surely your labors for Him ought to be more abundant than they used to be; but, alas, you do not look on it as a parallel case and so make excuses for yourself.

Too often in our spiritual work we fix our mind upon the differences rather than upon the similarities. For instance, David might have said, "I would not mind another lion, I can manage lions; I would not be afraid of half-a-dozen more bears, I am used to bears; but this Philistine is a new sort of monster." No, David saw it was the same thing after all, a little different in shape but the same brute force, and so he went at it with courage. But *we* say, "Alas, there is a great difference; our present trials have an unusual bitterness in them." "I," cries the widow, "I lost my husband, and God helped me, and my son has been a stay to me; but now he too is gone, and I have no other son, and no one to fall back upon." She points out the difference, though the trouble is virtually the same. Would it not be far better if she pleaded the same promise and believed in the Lord as she did before? One man will say, "Ah, yes, I did on such an occasion run all risks for God, but you see there is a difference here." I know there is, my dear brother, there is a little difference, and if you fix your eye on that, you will drill yourself into unbelief; but difference or no difference, where duty calls, danger will never be wanting there; and if you should be called to bear such an affliction as never befell mortal man before, yet remember God's arm is not shortened that He cannot deliver His servants, and you have but to commit yourself to Him, and out of the sevenfold adversity you shall come forth a sevenfold conqueror.

We are very apt, too, to look back upon the past and say, "I know that there are some grand things the Lord did for me, and my venture for His sake turned out well, but I do not know what I should have done if a happy circumstance had not occurred to help me just in the nick of time." We dare to attribute our deliverance to some very "happy accident." It is very base of us to do so, for it was the Lord who helped us from first to last, and the happy occurrence was a mere second cause; but cannot God give us another "happy accident" if necessary in this present trouble? Alas, unbelief says, "There was a circumstance in that case which really did alter it, and I cannot expect anything like that to occur now." Oh, how wrong this is of us! How we lose the force of that blessed reasoning from parallels which might have supplied us with courage! God grant we may break loose from this net.

Possibly our coward heart suggests, "Perhaps, after all, this deed of courage may not be quite my calling, and I had better not attempt it." David might have said, "I am a shepherd, and I can fight with lions, but I was never trained to war, and therefore I had better let this Philistine alone." He might also have discovered that he was better adapted for protecting sheep than for becoming the champion of a nation. We must guard against the use of this plausible pretext, for pretext it is. Brethren, if we have achieved success by the power of God, let us not dote upon some supposed adaptation but stand prepared to be used of the Lord in any other way which He may choose. Adaptation is unknown until the event proves it, and our Lord is a far better judge of that than we are. If you see before you a work by means of which you can glorify God and bless the church, do not hesitate, but enter upon it in reliance upon your God. Do not stand stuttering and stammering and talking about qualifications and so on, but what your hand finds to do, do it in the name of the Lord Jesus, who has bought you with His blood. Prove your qualifications by bringing Goliath's head back with you, and no further questions will be asked by anyone or by yourself.

So, too, sometimes we frame an excuse out of the opinions of others. We are apt to feel that we really must consider what other people say. Our good brother Eliab may be a little crusty in temper, but still he is a man of a good deal of prudence and experience, and he tells us to be quiet and let these things alone, and perhaps we had better do so. And there is Saul; well, he is a man of great acquaintance with such matters, and he judges that we had better decline the task, and therefore upon the whole we had better exhibit that prudence which is the better part of valor and not rush upon certain danger and probable destruction. This seeking advice and following cowardly counsel is all too common. We know that some strenuous effort is needed, and it is in our power, but we desire ease, and therefore we employ other men to weave excuses for us. It would be more honest to say outright that we do not want to do any more. Were we more full of love to Jesus, this unworthy device would be scorned by us, and in sacred manliness of mind we should scorn the counsel which tends to cowardice. Others cannot bear our responsibility; we must each one give all account of himself to God, why, then, yield to the judgments of men? Oh, brethren, fling this folly to the winds. Obey the dictates of the Holy Spirit, and close your ears to the advice of unbelief.

Men or women, consecrated to God, if the Lord impels you to do anything for Him, do not ask *me*, do not ask my fellow church officers, but go and do it. If God has helped you in the past, draw a parallel, and argue from it that He will help you in the present. Go, and the Lord go with you, but do not fall a prey to that wicked unbelief which would rob you of your strength.

Results

The results were, first, that David felt he would, as he did before, *rely upon God alone*. Come to the same resolution, brothers and sisters. God alone is the source of power; He alone can render real aid; let us then rest in Him, even if no other help appears. Is not the Lord alone enough? That arm which you cannot see will never be palsied; its sinews will never crack, but all the arms of mortals upon which you so much love to lean must one day turn to dust in the tomb; and while they live they are but weakness itself. Trust in the Lord forever, for in the Lord Jehovah there is everlasting strength. David had found wisdom's self when he said, "My soul wait thou only upon God, for my expectation is from him."

David resolved again *to run all risks once more*, as he had done before. As he had ventured himself against the lion, so he would put his life in His hand and engage the Philistine. Come wounds and maiming, come piercing spear or cutting sword, come death itself amid the taunts and exultations of his giant foe, he would still dare everything for Israel's sake and for God's sake. Soldiers of the Cross, if you feel that you can do this, be not slow to put it in practice; throw yourselves wholly into the Lord's service; consecrate yourselves, your substance, and all to the grand end of glorifying Christ, fighting against error and plucking souls from destruction.

David's next step was *to put himself into the same condition as on former occasions* by divesting himself of everything that hampered him. He had fought the lion with nature's weapons, and so would he meet the Philistine. Off went that glittering royal helmet, which no doubt made his head ache with its weight. Off went the cumbersome armor, in which he found it very hard to move. In such a metallic prison he did not feel like David a bit, and therefore he put all aside and wore only his shepherd's frock. As for that magnificent sword which he had just strapped by his side, he felt that it would be more ornament than use, and so he laid it aside with the rest of the trappings and put on his wallet and took nothing with him but his sling and stone. This was the old style, and he did well to keep to it, for the Lord saves not with sword and spear. We are all too apt to get into fine harness and tie ourselves up with rules and methods. The art of getting rid of all hamper is a noble one, but few have learned it. Look at our churches, look at the church at large, is there not enough red tape about to strangle a nation?

Have we not committees enough to sink a ship with their weight? As for patrons, presidents, vice-presidents, and secretaries, had not Christianity been divine it could not have lived under the load of these personages who sit on her bosom. The roundabouts are worrying straightforward action out of the world. We are organized into strait waistcoats. The vessel of the church has such an awful lot of top-hamper that I wonder how she can be navigated at all; and if a tempest were to come on, she would have to cut herself free from nearly all of it.

When shall we get at the work? If there should ever come a day when brethren will go forth preaching the Gospel, simply resting in faith upon the Lord alone, I for one expect to see grand results; but at present Saul's armor is everywhere. When we get rid of formality in preaching we shall see great results, but the churches are locked up in irons which they call armor. Why, dear me, if we are to have a special service, one brother must have it conducted on the Moody method, and another can only have Sankey hymns. Who, then, are we that we must follow others? Do not talk to us about innovations and all that; away with your rubbish! Let us serve God with all our hearts and preach Jesus Christ to sinners with our whole souls, and the mode is of no consequence. To preach down priestcraft and error and do it in the simplest possible manner by preaching up Christ is the way of wisdom. We must preach, not after the manner of doctors of divinity, but after the manner of those unlearned and ignorant men in the olden time who had been with Jesus and learned of Him. Brethren, some of you have too much armor on. Put it off; be simple, be natural, be artless, be plainspoken, be trustful in the living God, and you will succeed. Less of the artificer's brass and more of heaven-anointed manhood is wanted—more sanctified naturalness and less of studied artificialness. O Lord, send us this, for Christ's sake. Amen.

The ultimate result was that the young champion came back with Goliath's head in his hand, and equally sure triumphs await every one of you if you rely on the Lord and act in simple earnestness. If for Christ, my sister, you will go forward in His work, resting upon Him, you shall see souls converted by your instrumentality. If, my brother, you will but venture everything for Christ's glory and depend alone on Him, what men call fanaticism shall be considered by God to be only sacred consecration, and He will send you the reward which He always gives to a full, thorough, simple, unselfish faith in Himself.

If the result of my preaching this sermon should be to stir up half-a-dozen workers to some venturesome zeal for God, I shall greatly rejoice. I remember when I commenced this work in London. God being with me, I said if He would only give me half-a-dozen good men and women a work would be done, but that if I had half-a-dozen thousand sleepy people, nothing would be accomplished. At this time I am always afraid of our falling into a lethargic condition. This church numbers nearly five thousand members, but if you are only five thousand cowards, the battle will bring no glory to God. If we have one David among us, that one hero will do wonders; but think what an army would be if all the soldiers were Davids—it would be an ill case with the Philistines then. Oh that we were all Davids, that the weakest among us were as David, and David himself were better than he is and became like an angel of the Lord! God's Holy Spirit is equal to the doing of this, and why should He not do it? Let us call to Him for help, and that help will come.

I must just say this word to some here present who lament that there is nothing in this sermon for them. Unconverted persons, you cannot draw any argument from your past experience, for you have none of a right kind; but you may draw comfort, and I pray you do so, from another view of this story. Jesus Christ, the true David, has plucked some of us like lambs from between the jaws of the Devil. Many of us were carried captive by sin; transgression had so encompassed us about that we were unable to escape, but our great Lord delivered us. Sinner, why can He not deliver you? If you cannot fight the lion of the pit, He can. Do you ask me, What are you to do? Well, call for His help as loudly as you can. If you are like a lamb, bleat to Him, and the bleatings of the lamb will attract the Shepherd's ear. Cry mightily to the Lord for salvation, and trust alone in the Lord Jesus. He will save you. If you were between the jaws of hell, yet, if you believed in Him, He would surely pluck you out of destruction. God grant you may find it so, for Christ's sake. Amen.

7

A Greater Than Solomon

Behold, a greater than Solomon is here (Luke 11:31).

Our first thought is that no mere man would have said this concerning himself unless he had been altogether eaten up with vanity, for Solomon was among the Jews the very ideal of greatness and wisdom. It would be an instance of the utmost self-conceit if any mere man were to say of himself—"A greater than Solomon is here." Any person who was really greater and wiser than Solomon would be the last man to claim such preeminence. A wise man would never think it; a prudent man would never say it. The Lord Jesus Christ, if we regard Him as a mere man, would never have uttered such an expression, for a more modest, self-forgetting man was never found in all our race. View it on the supposition that the Christ of Nazareth was a mere man, and I say that His whole conduct was totally different from the spirit which would have suggested an utterance like this—"A greater than Solomon is here." For men to compare themselves with one another is not wise, and Christ was wise; it is not humble, and Christ was humble. He would not have thus spoken if there had not been cause and reason in His infinitely glorious nature. It was because the divinity within Him must speak out. For God to say that He is greater than all His creatures is no boasting, for what are they in His sight? All worlds are but sparks from the anvil of His omnipotence. Space, time, eternity, all these are as nothing before Him; and for Him to compare or even to contrast Himself with one of His own creatures is supreme condescension, let Him word the comparison how He may. It was the divine within our Lord which made Him say—and not even then with a view to exalt Himself but with a view to point the moral that He was trying to bring before the people—"A greater than

This sermon was taken from *The Metropolitan Tabernacle Pulpit* and was preached on Sunday evening, February 6, 1881.

Solomon is here." He did as good as say, "The queen of the south came from a distance to hear the wisdom of Solomon, but you refuse to hear *Me*. She gave attention to a man, but you will not regard your God. You will not listen to the incarnate Deity who tells you words of infinite, infallible wisdom." Our Lord Jesus is aiming at His hearers' good, and where the motive is so disinterested there remains no room for criticism. He tells them that He is greater than Solomon to convince them of the greatness of their crime in refusing to listen to the messages of love with which His lips were loaded. Foreigners came from afar to Solomon; but I, says He, have come to your door and brought infinite wisdom into your very gates, and yet you refuse Me. Therefore the queen of the south shall rise up in judgment against you, for, in rejecting Me, you reject a greater than Solomon.

The second thought that comes to one's mind is this: notice the self-consciousness of the Lord Jesus Christ.

He knows who He is and what He is, and He is not lowly in spirit because He is ignorant of His own greatness. He was meek and lowly in heart—*Servus servorum*, as the Latins were wont to call Him, "Servant of servants," but all the while He knew that He was *Rex regum*, or King of Kings. He takes a towel and He washes His disciples' feet; but all the while He knows that He is their Master and their Lord. He associates with publicans and harlots and dwells with the common people; but all the while He knows that He is the only begotten of the Father. He sits as a child in the temple hearing and asking questions of the rabbis; He stands among His disciples as though He were one of themselves, conversing with the ignorant and foolish of the day, seeking their good; but He knows that He is not one of them. He knows that He has nothing to learn from them. He knows that He is able to teach senates and to instruct kings and philosophers, for He is greater than Solomon. He wears a peasant's garb and has no where to lay His head; but He knows that, whatever the lowliness of His condition, He is greater than Solomon; He lets us perceive that He knows it, that all may understand the love which brought Him down so low. It is grand humility on Christ's part that He condescends to be our servant, our Savior, when He is so great that the greatest of men are as nothing before Him. "He counted it not robbery to be equal with God"; mark that; and yet "he made himself of no reputation." Some people do not know their own worth, and so, when they stoop to a lowly office it is no stoop to their minds, for they do not know their own abilities. They do not know to what they are equal; but Christ did know; He knew all about His own Deity and His own wisdom and greatness as man. I admire, therefore, the clear understanding which sparkles in His deep humiliation, like a gem in a dark mine. He is not one who stoops down according to the old rhyme—

As needs he must who cannot sit upright;

but He is one who comes down wittingly from His throne of glory, marking each step and fully estimating the descent which He is making. The cost of our redemption was known to Him, and He endured the Cross, despising the shame. Watts well sings—

> This was compassion like a God,
> That when the Savior knew
> The price of pardon was his blood,
> His pity ne'er withdrew.

Brethren, if our Savior Himself said that He was greater than Solomon, you and I must fully believe it, enthusiastically own it, and prepare to proclaim it. If others will not own it, let us be the more prompt to confess it. If He Himself had to say, before they would own it, "A greater than Solomon is here," let it not be necessary that the encomium should be repeated, but let us all confess that He is indeed greater than Solomon. Let us go home with this resolve in our minds, that we will speak greater things of Christ than we have done, that we will try to love Him more and serve Him better and make Him in our own estimation and in the world's greater than He has ever been. Oh for a glorious high throne to set Him on and a crown of stars to place upon His head! Oh to bring nations to His feet! I know my words cannot honor Him according to His merits—I wish they could. I am quite sure to fail in my own judgment when telling out His excellence indeed; I grow less and less satisfied with my thoughts and language concerning Him. He is too glorious for my feeble language to describe Him. If I could speak with the tongues of men and of angels, I could not speak worthily of Him. If I could borrow all the harmonies of heaven and enlist every harp and song of the glorified, yet were not the music sweet enough for His praises. Our glorious Redeemer is ever blessed; let us bless Him. He is to be extolled above the highest heavens; let us sound forth His praises. Oh for a well-tuned harp! May the Spirit of God help both heart and lip to extol Him at this hour.

First, then, we shall try to *draw a parallel between Jesus and Solomon*; and, secondly, we will break away from all comparisons and show where *there cannot be any parallel between Christ and Solomon at all*.

Between Christ and Solomon There Are Some Points of Likeness

When the Savior Himself gives us a comparison, it is a clear proof that a likeness was originally intended by the Holy Spirit, and therefore we may say without hesitation that Solomon was meant to be a type of Christ. I am not going into detail, nor am I about to refine upon small matters; but I shall give you five points in which Solomon was conspicuously like to Christ and in which our Lord was greater than Solomon. O for help in the great task before me.

And, first, in *wisdom*. Whenever you talked about Solomon to a Jew, his eyes began to flash with exultation; his blood leaped in his veins with national pride. Solomon—that name brought to mind the proudest time of David's dynasty, the age of gold. Solomon, the magnificent, why, surely, his name crowns Jewish history with glory, and the brightest beam of that glory is his wisdom. In the east, and I think I may say in the west, it still remains a proverb, "To be as wise as Solomon." No modern philosopher or learned monarch has ever divided the fame of the son of David, whose name abides as the synonym of wisdom. Of no man since could it be said as of him, "And all the kings of the earth sought the presence of Solomon to bear his wisdom, that God had put in his heart." *He intermeddled with all knowledge* and was a master in all sciences. He was a naturalist: "and he spake of trees, from the cedar trees that are in Lebanon even unto the hyssop that springeth out of the wall: he spake also of beasts, and of fowl, and of creeping things, and of fishes." He was an engineer and architect, for he wrote: "I made me great works; I builded me houses; I planted me vineyards: I made me gardens and orchards, and I planted trees in them of all kind of fruits; I made me pools of water, to water therewith the wood that bringeth forth trees." He was one who understood the science of government—a politician of the highest order. He was everything, in fact. God gave him wisdom and largeness of heart, says the Scripture, like the sand of the sea: "and Solomon's wisdom excelled the wisdom of all the children of the east country, and all the wisdom of Egypt. For he was wiser than all men; than Ethan the Ezrahite, and Heman, and Chalcol, and Darda, the sons of Mahol: and his fame was in all nations round about."

Yes; but our Savior knows infinitely more than Solomon. I want you tonight to come to Him just as the Queen of Sheba came to Solomon, only for weightier reasons. You do not want to learn anything concerning architecture or navigation, agriculture or anatomy. You want to know only how you shall be built up a spiritual house and how you shall cross those dangerous seas which lie between this land and the celestial city. Well, you may come to Jesus and He will teach you all that you need to know, for all wisdom is in Christ. Our divine Savior knows things past and present and future; the secrets of God are with Him. He knows the inmost heart of God, for no one knows the Father save the Son and He to whom the Son shall reveal Him. To Him it is given to take the book of prophetic decree and loose the seven seals thereof.

Come, then, to Christ Jesus if you want to know the mind of God, for it is written that He "is made unto us wisdom." Solomon might have wisdom, but he could not be wisdom to others; Christ Jesus is that to the full. In the multifarious knowledge which He possesses—the universal knowledge which is stored up in Him—there is enough for your guidance and instruction even to the end of life, however intricate and overshadowed your path may be.

Solomon proved his wisdom in part by his *remarkable inventions*. We cannot tell what Solomon did not know. At any rate, no man knows at this present moment how those huge stones, which have lately been discovered, which were the basis of the ascent by which Solomon went up to the house of the Lord, were ever put into their places. Many of the stones of Solomon's masonry are so enormous that scarcely could any modern machinery move them; and without the slightest cement they are put together so exactly that the blade of a knife could not be inserted between them. It is marvelous how the thing was done. How such great stones were brought from their original bed in the quarry—how the whole building of the temple was executed—nobody knows. The castings in brass and silver are scarcely less remarkable. No doubt many inventions have passed away from the knowledge of modern times, inventions as remarkable as those of our own age. We are a set of savages that are beginning to learn something, but Solomon knew and invented things which we shall, perhaps, rediscover in five hundred years time. By vehement exertion this boastful nineteenth century, wretched century as it is, will crawl toward the wisdom which Solomon possessed ages ago.

Yet is Jesus greater than Solomon. As for inventions, Solomon is no inventor at all compared with Him who said, "Deliver him from going down into the pit, for I have found a ransom." O Savior, did You find out the way of our salvation? Did You bring into the world and carry out and execute the way by which hell-gate should be closed, and heaven-gate, once barred, should be set wide open? Then, indeed, are You wiser than Solomon. You are the devisor of salvation, the architect of the church, the author and finisher of our faith.

Solomon has left us some very *valuable books*—the Proverbs, Ecclesiastes, and the matchless Song. But, oh, the words of Solomon fall far short of the words of Jesus Christ, for they are spirit and life. The power of the word of Jesus is infinitely greater than all the deep sayings of the sage. Proverbial wisdom cannot match His sayings, nor can "The Preacher" rival His sermons, and even the divine Song itself would remain without a meaning—an allegory never to be explained—if it were not that Christ Himself is the sum and substance of it. Solomon may sing of Christ, but Christ is the substance of the Song.

He is greater than Solomon in His teachings, for His wisdom is from above and leads men up to heaven. Blessed are they that sit at His feet.

Again, Solomon showed his wisdom in *difficult judgments.* You know how he settled the question between the two women concerning the child; many other puzzles Solomon solved, and many other knots Solomon was able to untie. He was a great ruler and governor—a man wise in politics, in social economy, and in commerce—wise in all human respects. But a greater than Solomon is present where Christ is. There is no difficulty which Christ cannot remove, no knot which He cannot untie, no question which He cannot answer. You may bring your hard questions to Him, and He will answer them. If you have any difficulty on your heart tonight, do but resort to the Lord Jesus Christ in prayer, and search His Word, and you shall hear a voice as from the sacred oracle, which shall lead you in the path of safety.

My point at this time, especially as we are coming to the Communion Table, is this. I want you that love the Lord Jesus Christ to believe in His infinite wisdom and come to Him for direction. I fear that when you are in trouble, you half suppose that the great keeper of Israel must have made a mistake. You get into such an intricate path that you say, "Surely, my Shepherd has not guided me aright." Never think so. When you are poor and needy still say, "This my poverty was ordained by a greater than Solomon." What if you seem to be deprived of every comfort, and you are brought into a strange and solitary way where you find no city to dwell in? Yet a guide is near, and that guide is not foolish; but a greater than Solomon is here. I think I look tonight into a great furnace. It is so fierce that I cannot bear to gaze into its terrible blaze. For fear my eyeballs should utterly fail me and lose the power of sight through the glare of that tremendous flame, I turn aside, for the fury of its flame overpowers me. But when I am strengthened to look again, I see ingots of silver refining in the white heat, and I note that the heat is tempered to the last degree of nicety. I watch the process to the end, and I say, as I behold those ingots brought out all clear and pure, refined from all dross and ready for the heavenly treasury, "Behold, a greater than Solomon was in that furnace work." So you will find it, O sufferer. Infinite wisdom is in your lot. Come, poor child, do not begin to interfere with your Savior's better judgment, but let it order all things. Do not let your little "Know" ever rise up against the great knowledge of your dear Redeemer. Think of this when you wade in deep waters, and comfortably whisper to yourself—"A greater than Solomon is here."

I have not time to enlarge, and therefore I would have you notice, next, that our Lord Jesus Christ is greater than Solomon in *wealth.* This was one of the things for which Solomon was noted. He had great treasures; he "made gold to be as stones, and as for silver it was little accounted of," so rich did he become. He had multitudes of servants. I think he had sixty thousand hewers in the mountains hewing out stones and wood, so numerous were the workmen he employed. His court was magnificent to the last degree. When you read of the victuals that were prepared to feed the court and of the stately way in which every thing was arranged from the stables of the horses upward to the ivory throne, you feel, like the Queen of Sheba, utterly astonished, and say, "The half was not told me."

But, oh, when you consider all the wealth of Solomon, what poor stuff it is compared with the riches that are treasured up in Christ Jesus. Beloved, He who died upon the cross and was indebted to a friend for a grave, He who was stripped even to the last rag before He died, He who possessed no wealth but that of sorrow and sympathy yet had about Him the power to make many rich, and He has made multitudes rich— rich to all the intents of everlasting bliss; and therefore He must be rich Himself. Is He not rich who enriches millions? Why, our Lord Jesus Christ, even by a word, comforted those that were bowed down. When He stretched out His hand, He healed the sick with a touch. There was a wealth about His every movement. He was a full man, full of all that man could desire to be full of; and now, seeing that He has died and risen again, there is in Him a wealth of pardoning love, a wealth of saving power, a wealth of intercessory might before the Father's throne, a wealth of all things by which He enriches the sons of men and shall enrich them to all eternity.

I want this truth to come home to you; I want you to recognize the riches of Christ, you that are His people; and, in addition, to remember the truth of our hymn—

> Since Christ is rich can I be poor?
> What can I want besides?

I wish we could learn to reckon what we are by what Christ is. An old man said, "I am very old; I have lost my only son. I am penniless; and, worst of all, I am blind. But," added he, "this does not matter, for Christ is not infirm; Christ is not aged; Christ has all riches. Christ is not blind, and Christ is mine, and I have all things in Him." Could you not get hold of that somehow, brothers and sisters? Will not the Holy Spirit teach you the art of appropriating the Lord Jesus and all that He is and has? If Christ be your representative, why, then you are rich in Him. Go to Him to be enriched. Suppose I were to meet a woman and I knew her husband to be a very wealthy man and that he loved her very much, and she were to say to me, "I am dreadfully poor; I do not know where to get raiment and food." "Oh," I should say, "That woman is out of her mind." If she has such a husband, surely she has only to go to him for all that she needs. And what if nothing is invested in her name, yet it is in his name, and they are one, and he will deny her nothing. I should say, "My good woman, you must not talk in that fashion, or I will tell your husband of you." Well, I think that I shall have to say the same of you who are so very poor and cast down and yet are married to Jesus Christ. I shall have to tell your Husband of you, that you bring such complaints against Him, for all things are yours, for you are Christ's and Christ is God's; wherefore, "lift up the hands that hang down, and confirm the feeble knees"; use the knees of prayer and the hand of faith, and your estate will well content you. Do not think that you are married to Rehoboam, who will beat you with scorpions, for you are joined to a greater than Solomon. Do not fancy that your heavenly Bridegroom is a beggar. All the wealth of eternity and infinity is His; how can you say that you are poor while all that He has is yours?

Now, thirdly, and very briefly indeed. There was one point about Solomon in which every Israelite rejoiced, namely, that he was *the prince of peace*. His name signifies peace. His father, David, was a great warrior, but Solomon had not to carry on war. His power was such that no one dared to venture upon a conflict with so great and potent a monarch. Every man throughout Israel sat under his vine and fig tree, and no man was afraid. No trumpet of invader was heard in the land. Those were halcyon days for Israel when Solomon reigned.

Ah, but in that matter a greater than Solomon is here; for Solomon could not give his subjects peace of mind; he could not bestow upon them rest of heart; he could not ease them of their burden of guilt or draw the arrow of conviction from their breast and heal its smart. But I preach to you tonight that blessed divine Man of Sorrows who has wrought out our redemption and who is greater than Solomon in His peace-giving power. Oh, come and trust Him. Then shall your "peace be as a river, and your righteousness like the waves of the sea." Am I addressing one of God's people who is sorely troubled, tumbled up and down in his thoughts? Brother or sister, do not think that you must wait a week or two before you can recover your peace. You can become restful in a moment, for "He is our peace"—even He Himself, and He alone. And, oh, if you will but take Him at once, laying hold upon Him by the hand of faith as your Savior, this man shall be the peace even when the Assyrian shall come into the land. There is no peace like the peace which Jesus gives; it is like a river, deep, profound, renewed, ever flowing, overflowing, increasing and widening into an ocean of bliss. "The peace of God, which passes all understanding, shall keep your heart and mind, through Jesus Christ." Oh, come to Him. Come to Him at this moment. Do not remain an hour away from your Noah, or rest, for with Him in the ark your weary wing shall be tired no longer. You shall be safe and restful the moment you return to Him. The fruit of the Spirit is joy. I want you to get that joy and to enter into this peace. Blessed combination, joy and peace! Peace, peace, there is music in the very word. Get it from Him who is the Word, and whose voice can still a storm into a calm. A greater than Solomon is here to give you that peace; beat the sword of your inward warfare into the plowshare of holy service; no longer sound an alarm, but blow up the trumpet of peace in this the day of peace.

A fourth thing for which Solomon was noted was his *great works*. Solomon built the temple, which was one of the seven wonders of the world at its time. A very marvelous building it must have been, but I will not stay to describe it, for time fails us. In addition to this he erected for himself palaces, constructed fortifications, and made aqueducts and great pools to bring streams from the mountains to the various towns. He also founded Palmyra and Baalbee—those cities of the desert—to facilitate his commerce with India, Arabia, and other remote regions. He was a marvelous man. Earth has not seen his like.

And yet a greater than Solomon is here, for Christ has brought the living water from the throne of God right down to thirsty men, being Himself the eternal aqueduct through which the heavenly current streams. Christ has built fortresses and munitions of defense behind which His children stand secure against the wrath of hell. He has founded and is daily finishing a wondrous temple, His church, of which His people are the living stones, fashioned, polished, rendered beautiful—a temple which God Himself shall inhabit, for He "dwelleth not in temples made with hands, that is to say, of this building"; but He dwells in a temple which He Himself does pile, of which Christ is architect and builder, foundation and chief cornerstone. But Jesus builds for eternity, an everlasting temple, and, when all visible things pass away and the very ruins of Solomon's temple and Solomon's aqueduct are scarcely to be discerned, what a sight will be seen in that New Jerusalem! The twelve courses of its foundations are of precious stones; its walls bedight with diamonds rare; its streets are paved with gold, and its glory surpasses that of the sun. I am but talking figures, poor figures, too; for the glory of the city of God is spiritual, and where shall I find words with which to depict it? There, where the Lamb Himself is the light and the Lord God Himself does dwell—there the whole edifice, the entire New Jerusalem—shall be to the praise and the glory of His grace who gave Jesus Christ to be the builder of the house of His glory, of which I hope we shall form a part forever and ever.

Now, if Christ does such great works, I want you to come to Him, that He may work in you the work of God. That is the point. Come and trust Him at once. Trust Him to build you up. Come and trust Him to bring the living water to your lips. Come and trust Him to make you a temple of the living God. Come, dear child of God, if you have great works to do, come and ask for the power of Christ with which to perform them. Come, you that would leave some memorial to the honor of the divine name, come to Him to teach and strengthen you. He is the wise Master-builder; come and be workers together with Christ. Baptize your weakness into His infinite strength, and you shall be strong in the Lord and in the power of His might. God help you so to do.

Once more. I draw the parallel upon the fifth point, and I have done with it. Solomon was great as to *dominion*. The kingdom of the Jews was never anything like the size before or after that Solomon made it. It appears to have extended from the river of Egypt right across the wilderness far up to the Persian Gulf. We can scarcely tell how far Solomon's dominions reached; they are said to have been "from sea to sea, and from the river even unto the ends of the earth." By one mode or another he managed to bring various kings into subjection to him, and he was the greatest monarch that ever swayed the scepter of Judah. It has all gone now. Poor, feeble Rehoboam dropped from his foolish hands the reins his father held. The kingdom was rent in pieces; the tributary princes found their liberty, and the palmy days of Israel were over.

On the contrary, our Lord Jesus Christ at this moment has dominion over all things. God has set Him over all the works of His hands. Aye, tell it out among the heathen that the Lord reigns. The feet that were nailed to the tree are set upon the necks of His enemies. The hands that bore the nails sway at this moment the scepter of all worlds—Jesus is King of Kings and Lord of Lords! Hallelujah! Let universal sovereignty be ascribed to the Son of Man, to Him who was "despised and rejected of men, a man of sorrows and acquainted with grief." Tell it out, you saints, for your own comfort. The Lord reigns, let the earth rejoice, let the multitude of the isles be glad thereof. Everything that happens in providence is under His sway still, and the time is coming when a moral and spiritual kingdom will be set up by Him which shall encompass the whole world.

It does not look like it, does it? All these centuries have passed away, and little progress has been made. Ah, but He comes; and when He comes, or before He comes, He shall overturn, overturn, overturn, for His right it is, and God will give it Him. And, as surely as God lives, to Him shall every man bow the knee, "and every tongue shall confess that Jesus Christ is Lord, to the glory of God the Father." Do not be afraid about it. Do not measure difficulties, much less tremble at them. What is faith made for but to believe that which seems impossible? To expect universal dominion for Christ when everything goes well is but the expectation of reason; but to expect it when everything goes ill is the triumph of Abrahamic confidence. Look upon the great mountain and say, "Who are you, O great mountain? Before the true Zerubbabel you shall become a plain." In the blackest midnight, when the ebony darkness stands thick and hard as granite before you, believe that, at the mystic touch of Christ, the whole of it shall pass away, and at the brightness of His rising the eternal light shall dawn, never to be quenched. This is to act the part of a believer; and I ask you to act that part and believe to the full in Christ the Omnipotent. What means this stinted faith in an almighty arm? What a fidget we are in and what a worry seizes us if a little delay arises! Everything has to be done in the next ten minutes, or we count our Lord to be slack. Is this the part of wisdom? The Eternal has infinite leisure, who are we that we should hasten Him?

> His purposes will ripen fast,
> Unfolding every hour.

A day is long to us, but a thousand years to Him are but as the twinkling of a star. Oh, rest in the Lord, and wait patiently for Him, for the time shall come when the God of Israel shall put to rout His adversaries, and the Christ of the cross shall be the Christ of the crown. We shall one day hear it said—The great Shepherd reigns; and His unsuffering kingdom now has come. Then rocks and hills and vales and islands of the sea shall all be vocal with the one song, "Worthy is the Lamb that was slain to receive honor and glory and power and dominion and might forever and ever!"

Thus I have tried to draw the parallel, but I pray you to see the Lord Jesus for yourself and know whether I have spoken the truth about Him. You have heard the report; now, like the Queen of Sheba, go and see for yourself. Get to Christ, as to His dominion, come under His sway and own His scepter. Go and trust your King; love your King; praise your King; delight in your King. How courtiers delight to be summoned to court! How glad they are to see the queen's face. How pleased they are if she gives them but a kindly word! Surely, their fortune is made, or at least their hopes are raised and their spirits lifted up. Shall we not sun ourselves in the presence of the blessed and only Potentate? Let us come into the presence of our King tonight, or else let us sit here and weep. Let us come to His table to feed upon Himself. Let us live on His Word. Let us delight in His love; and we shall surely say, "A greater than Solomon is here."

Between Christ and Solomon There Is Much More Contrast Than Comparison

I shall not detain you longer than a minute or two while I remark that we must rise beyond all parallels, if we would reach the height of this great argument, for between Christ and Solomon there is much more contrast than comparison—much more difference than likeness.

In His *nature* the Lord Jesus is greater than Solomon. Alas, poor Solomon! The strongest man that ever lived, namely, Samson, was the weakest of men; and the wisest man that ever lived was, perhaps, the greatest, certainly the most conspicuous, fool. How different is our Lord! There is no infirmity in Christ, no folly in the incarnate God. The backsliding of Solomon finds no parallel in Jesus, in whom the prince of this world found nothing though he searched Him through and through.

Our Lord is greater than Solomon because He is not mere man. He is man, perfect man, man to the utmost of manhood, sin excepted; but still He is more, and infinitely more, than man. "In him dwelleth all the fullness of the Godhead bodily." He is God Himself. "The Word was God." God dwells in Him, and He Himself is God.

As in nature He was infinitely superior to Solomon and not to be compared with him for a moment, so was He in *character.* Look at Christ and Solomon for a minute as to real greatness of character, and you can hardly see Solomon with a microscope, while Christ rises grandly before you, growing every moment until He fills the whole horizon of your admiration. Principally let me note the point of self-sacrifice. Jesus lived entirely for other people; He had never a thought about Himself. Solomon was, to a great extent, wise to himself, rich to himself, strong to himself; and you see in those great palaces and in all their arrangements that he seeks his own pleasure, honor, and emolument; and, alas! that seeking of pleasure leads him into sin, that sin into a still greater one. Solomon, wonderful as he is, only compels you to admire him for his greatness, but you do not admire him for his goodness. You see nothing that makes you love him; you rather tremble before him than feel gladdened by him.

Oh, but look at Christ. He does not have a thought for Himself. He lives for others. How grandly magnificent He is in disinterested love. He "loved his church and gave himself for it." He pours out even His heart's blood for the good of men; and hence, dear friends, at this moment our blessed Lord is infinitely superior to Solomon in His *influence.* Solomon has little or no influence today. Even in his own time he never commanded the influence that Christ had in His deepest humiliation. I do not hear of any that were willing to die for Solomon; certainly nobody would do so now. But how perpetually is enthusiasm kindled in ten thousand breasts for Christ! They say that if again there were stakes in Smithfield, we should not find men to burn at them for Christ. I tell you, it is not so. The Lord Jesus Christ has at this moment a remnant according to the election of His grace who would fling themselves into a pit of fire for Him and joy to do it. "Who shall separate us"—even us poor pigmies—"from the love of God which is in Christ Jesus our Lord?" "Oh," says one, "I do not think I could suffer martyrdom." You are not yet called to do so, my brother, and God has not given you the strength to do it before the need arises; but you will have strength enough if ever it comes to your lot to die for Jesus. Did you never hear of the martyr who, the night before he was to be burned, sat opposite the fire, and, taking his shoe off, held his foot close to the flame until he began to feel the burning of it? He drew it back and said, "I see God does not give me power to bear such suffering as I put upon myself, but I make nonetheless doubt," said he, "that I shall very well stand the stake tomorrow morning and burn quick to the death for Christ without starting back." And so he did, for he was noticed never to stir at all while the flames were consuming him.

There is a great deal of difference between your strength today and what your strength would be if you were called to some tremendous work or suffering. My Lord and Master, let me tell you, wakes more enthusiasm in human breasts at this moment than any other name in the universe. Napoleon once said, "I founded a kingdom upon force, and it will pass away"; but "Christ founded a kingdom upon love, and it will last forever and ever." And so it will. Blot out the name of Christ from the hearts of His people? Strike yon sun from the firmament and quench the stars; and when you have achieved that easy task, yet have you not begun to remove the glory of the indwelling Christ from the hearts of His people. Some of us delight to think that we bear in our body the marks of the Lord Jesus. "Where?" says one. I answer, it is all over us. We have been buried into His name, and we belong to Him in spirit, soul, and body. That watermark, which denotes that we are His, can never be taken out of us. We are dead with Him, wherein also we were buried with Him and are risen again with Him; and there is nothing at this moment that stirs our soul like the name of Jesus. Speak for yourselves. Is it not so? Have you never heard of one who lay dying, his mind wandering, and his wife said to him, "My dear, do you not know me?" He shook his head; and they brought near his favorite child. "Do you not know me?" He shook his head. One whispered, "Do you know the Lord Jesus Christ?" and he said, "He is all my salvation and all my desire." Oh, blessed name! Blessed name!

Some years ago I was away from this place for a little rest, and I was thinking to myself, "Now, I wonder whether I really respond to the power of the Gospel as I should like to do? I will go and hear a sermon and see." I would like to sit down with you in the pews sometimes and hear somebody else preach—not everybody, mark you, for when I hear a good many I want to be doing it myself. I get tired of them if they do not glow and burn. But that morning I thought I would drop into a place of worship such as there might be in the little town. A poor, plain man, a countryman, began preaching about Jesus Christ. He praised my Master in very humble language, but he praised Him most sincerely. Oh, but the tears began to flow. I soon laid the dust all around me where I sat, and I thought, "Bless the Lord! I do love Him." It only wants somebody else to play the harp instead of me, and my soul is ready to dance to the heavenly tune. Only let the music be Christ's sweet, dear, precious name, and my heart leaps at the sound. Oh, my brethren, sound out the praises of Jesus Christ! Sound out that precious name! There is none like it under heaven to stir my heart. I hope you can all say the same. I know you can if you love Him, for all renewed hearts are enamored of the sweet Lord Jesus. "A greater than Solomon is here." Solomon has no power over your hearts, but Jesus has. His influence is infinitely greater; His *power to bless* is infinitely greater; and so let us magnify and adore Him with all our hearts.

Oh, that all loved Him! Alas that so many do not! What strange monsters! Why, if you do not love Christ, what are you at? You hearts of stone, will you not break? If His dying love does not break them, what will? If you cannot see the beauties of Jesus, what can you see? You blind bats! O you that know not the music of His name, you are deaf. O you that do not rejoice in Him, you are dead. What are you at, that you are spared through the pleadings of His love and yet do not love Him? God have mercy upon you and bring you to delight yourselves in Christ and trust Him! As for us who do trust Him, we mean to love Him and delight in Him more and more, world without end. Amen.

8

Obadiah; or, Early Piety Eminent Piety

I thy servant fear the Lord from my youth (1 Kings 18:12).

I suspect that Elijah did not think very much of Obadiah. He does not treat him with any great consideration but addresses him more sharply than one would expect from a fellow believer. Elijah was the man of action—bold, always to the front, with nothing to conceal; Obadiah was a quiet believer, true and steadfast, but in a very difficult position, and therefore driven to perform his duty in a less open manner. His faith in the Lord swayed his life but did not drive him out of the court. I notice that even after Elijah had learned more of him at this interview, he speaks concerning God's people as if he did not reckon much upon Obadiah and others like him. He says, "They have thrown down thine altars, and slain thy prophets with the sword; and I, even I only, am left; and they seek my life, to take it away." He knew very well that Obadiah was left, who, though not exactly a prophet, was a man of mark; but he seems to ignore him as if he were of small account in the great struggle. I suppose it was because this man of iron, this prophet of fire and thunder, this mighty servant of the Most High set small store by anybody who did not come to the front and fight like himself.

I know it is the tendency of brave and zealous minds somewhat to undervalue quiet, retired piety. True and accepted servants of God may be doing their best under great disadvantages, against fierce opposition, but they may scarcely be known and may even shun the least recognition; therefore men who live in the fierce light of public life are apt to underestimate them. These minor stars are lost in the brilliance of the

This sermon was taken from *The Metropolitan Tabernacle Pulpit* and was preached on Sunday morning, October 19, 1884.

man whom God lights up like a new sun to flame through the darkness. Elijah flashed over the sky of Israel like a thunderbolt from the hand of the Eternal, and naturally he would be somewhat impatient of those whose movements were slower and less conspicuous. It is Martha and Mary over again, in some respects.

The Lord does not love that His servants, however great they are, should think lightly of their lesser comrades, and it occurs to me that He so arranged matters that Obadiah became important to Elijah when he had to face the wrathful king of Israel. The prophet is bidden to go and show himself to Ahab, and he does so; but he judges it better to begin by showing himself to the governor of his palace that he may break the news to his master and prepare him for the interview. Ahab was exasperated by the terrible results of the long drought and might in his sudden fury attempt to kill the prophet; and so he is to have time for consideration, that he may cool down a little.

Elijah has an interview with Obadiah and bids him go and say to Ahab, "Behold Elijah." It may sometimes be the nearest way to our object to go a little round about. But it is remarkable that Obadiah should thus be made useful to a man so much his superior. He who never feared the face of kings nevertheless found himself using as his helper a far more timid individual. The Lord may put you, my dear brother, who are so eminent, so useful, so brave, perhaps, so severe, into a position in which the humbler and more retiring believer, who has not half the grace nor half the courage that you have, may, nevertheless, become important to your mission. When He does this, He would have you learn the lesson, and learn it well, that the Lord has a place for all His servants and that He would not have us despise the least of them, but value them and cherish the good that is in them. The head must not say to the foot, I have no need of you. Those members of the mystical body which are weakest are yet necessary to the whole fabric. The Lord does not despise the day of small things, neither will He have His people do so. Elijah must not deal harshly with Obadiah. I would that Obadiah had had more courage. I wish that he had testified for the Lord, his God, as openly as Elijah did; but still every man in his own order; to his own master every servant must stand or fall. All lights are not moons, some are only stars; and even one star differs from another star in glory. God has His praise out of the least known of the holy characters of Scripture, even as the night has its light out of those glimmering bodies which cannot be discerned as separate stars but are portions of nebulous masses in which myriads of far-off lights are melted into one.

We learn further from the narrative before us that God will never leave Himself without witnesses in this world. Aye, and He will not leave Himself without witnesses in the worst places of the world. What a horrible abode for a true believer Ahab's court must have been! If there had been no sinner there but that woman Jezebel, she was enough to make the palace a sink of iniquity. That strong-minded, proud, Sidonian Queen twisted poor Ahab round her fingers just as she pleased. He might never have been the persecutor he was if his wife had not stirred him up; but she hated the worship of Jehovah intensely and despised the homeliness of Israel in comparison with the more pompous style of Sidon. Ahab must yield to her imperious demands, for she would brook no contradiction, and when her proud spirit was roused, she defied all opposition. Yet in that very court where Jezebel was mistress, the chamberlain was a man who feared God greatly. Never be surprised to meet with a believer anywhere. Grace can live where you would never expect to see it survive for an hour.

Joseph feared God in the court of Pharaoh; Daniel was a trusted counselor of Nebuchadnezzar; Mordecai waited at the gate of Ahasuerus; Pilate's wife pleaded for the life of Jesus, and there were saints in Caesar's household. Think of finding diamonds of the first water on such a dunghill as Nero's palace. Those who feared God in Rome were not only Christians, but they were examples to all other Christians for their brotherly love and generosity. Surely there is no place in this land where there is not some light; the darkest cavern of iniquity has its torch. Be not afraid; you may find followers of Jesus in the precincts of Pandemonium. In the palace of Ahab you meet an Obadiah who rejoices to hold fellowship with despised saints and quits the levees of a monarch for the hiding places of persecuted ministers.

I notice that these witnesses for God are very often persons converted in their youth. He seems to take a delight to make these his special standard-bearers in the day of battle. Look at Samuel! When all Israel became disgusted with the wickedness of Eli's sons, the child Samuel ministered before the Lord. Look at David! When he is but a shepherd boy, he wakes the echoes of the lone hills with his psalms and the accompanying music of his harp. See Josiah! When Israel had revolted, it was a child, Josiah by name, that broke down the altars of Baal and burned the bones of his priests. Daniel was but a youth when he took his stand for purity and God. The Lord has today—I know not where—some little Luther on his mother's knee, some young Calvin learning in our Sunday school, some youthful Zwingli singing a hymn to Jesus. This age may grow worse and worse; I sometimes think it will, for many signs look that way; but the Lord is preparing for it. The days are dark and ominous; and this eventide may darken down into a blacker night than has been known before; but God's cause is safe in God's hands. His work will not tarry for want of men. Put not forth the hand of Uzzah to steady the ark of the Lord; it shall go safely on in

God's predestined way. Christ will not fail nor be discouraged. God buries His workmen, but His work lives on. If there is not in the palace a king who honors God, there shall yet be found there a governor who fears the Lord from his youth, who shall take care of the Lord's prophets and hide them away until better days shall come. Wherefore be of good courage, and look for happier hours. Nothing of real value is in jeopardy while Jehovah is on the throne. The Lord's reserves are coming up, and their drums beat victory.

Concerning Obadiah I wish to speak with you this morning. His piety is the subject of discourse; we wish to use it for stimulating the zeal of those who teach the young.

Early Piety

First, we shall notice that Obadiah possessed early piety—"I thy servant fear the Lord from my youth." Oh that all our youth who may grow up to manhood and womanhood may be able to say the same. Happy are the people who are in such a case!

How Obadiah came to fear the Lord in youth we cannot tell. The instructor by whom he was led to faith in Jehovah is not mentioned. Yet we may reasonably conclude that he had believing parents. Slender as the ground may seem to be, I think it is pretty firm when I remind you of *his name*. This would very naturally be given him by his father or his mother, and as it signifies "the servant of Jehovah," I should think it indicated his parents' piety. In the days when there was persecution everywhere against the faithful and the name of Jehovah was in contempt because the calves of Bethel and the images of Baal were set up everywhere, I do not think that unbelieving parents would have given to their child the name of "the servant of Jehovah" if they themselves had not felt a reverence for the Lord. They would not idly have courted the remarks of their idolatrous neighbors and the enmity of the great. In a time when names meant something, they would have called him "the child of Baal" or "the servant of Chemosh" or some other name expressive of reverence to the popular gods, if the fear of God had not been before their eyes. The selection of such a name betrays to me their earnest desire that their boy might grow up to serve Jehovah and never bow his knee before the abhorred idols of the Sidonian Queen. Whether this be so or not, it is quite certain that thousands of the most intelligent believers owe their first bent toward godliness to the sweet associations of home.

How many of us might well have borne some such a name as that of Obadiah, for no sooner did we see the light than our parents tried to enlighten us with the truth. We were consecrated to the service of God before we knew that there was a God. Many a tear of earnest prayer fell

on our infant brow and sealed us for heaven. We were nursed in the atmosphere of devotion. There was scarce a day in which we were not
urged to be faithful servants of God and entreated while we were yet
young to seek Jesus and give our hearts to him. Oh, what we owe,
many of us, to the providence which gave us such a happy parentage!
Blessed be God for His great mercy to the children of His chosen!

If he had no gracious parents, I cannot tell how Obadiah came to be
a believer in the Lord in those sad days, unless he fell in with some
kind teacher, tender nurse, perhaps a good servant in his father's house,
or a pious neighbor, who dared to gather little children round about him
and tell of the Lord God of Israel. Some holy woman may have in-
stilled the law of the Lord into his young mind before the priests of
Baal could poison him with their falsehoods. No mention is made of
anybody in connection with this man's conversion in his youth, and it
does not matter, does it? You and I do not want to be mentioned if we
are right-hearted servants of God. Not to us be the glory. If souls are
saved, God has the honor of it. He knows what instrument He used, and
as He knows it, that is enough. The favor of God is fame enough for a
believer. All the blasts of fame's brazen trumpet are but so much wasted
wind compared with that one sentence from the mouth of God, "Well
done, good and faithful servant." Go on, dear teachers, since you are
called to the sacred ministry of instructing the young; do not grow
weary of it. Go on, though you may be unknown, for your seed sown in
the darkness shall be reaped in the light. You may be teaching an
Obadiah, whose name shall be heard in future years; you are providing
a father for the church and a benefactor for the world. Though your
name be forgotten, your work shall not be. When that illustrious day
shall dawn, compared with which all other days are dim, when the unknown shall be made known to the assembled universe, what you have
spoken in darkness shall be declared in the light.

If it was not in this way that Obadiah was brought to fear the Lord in
his youth, we may think of methods such as the Lord devises for the
bringing in of his banished. I have been very pleased lately, when I
have been seeing inquirers, to talk with several young persons who
have come out from utterly worldly families. I put to them the question,
"Is your father a member of a Christian church?" The answer has been
a shake of the head. "Does he attend a place of worship?" "No, sir, I
never knew him to go to one." "Your mother?" "Mother does not care
about religion." "Have you any brother or sister like-minded with yourself?" "No, sir." "Have you any single relative who knows the Lord?"
"No, sir." "Were you brought up by anyone who led you to attend the
means of grace and urged you to believe on the Lord Jesus?" "No, sir,
and yet from my childhood I have always had a desire to know the

Lord." Is it not remarkable that it should be so? What a wonderful proof of the election of grace! Here is one taken out of a family while all the rest are left, what say you to this? Here is one called in early childhood and prompted by the secret whispers of the Spirit of God to seek after the Lord while all the rest of the family slumber in midnight darkness. If that is your case, dear friend, magnify the sovereignty of God and adore Him as long as you live, for "he will have mercy on whom he will have mercy."

Still, I take it, the major part of those who come to know the Lord in their youth are persons who have had the advantage of godly parents and holy training. Let us persevere in the use of those means which the Lord ordinarily uses, for this is the way of wisdom and duty.

This early piety of Obadiah's *had special marks of genuineness about it*. The way in which he described it is, to my mind, very instructive, "I thy servant *fear the Lord* from my youth." I hardly remember in all my life to have heard the piety of children described in ordinary conversation by this term, though it is the common word of the Scriptures. We say, "The dear child loved God." We talk of their "being made so happy," and so forth, and I do not question the rightness of the language; still, the Holy Spirit speaks of "the fear of the Lord as the beginning of wisdom"; and David says, "Come, ye children, hearken unto me: I will teach you the fear of the Lord." Children will get great joy through faith in the Lord Jesus; but that joy, if true, is full of lowly reverence and awe of the Lord. Joy may be the sweet fruit of the Spirit, but it also may be an excitement of the flesh; for you remember that they upon the stony ground, which had not much depth of earth, received the word with joy, and the seed sprang up immediately; but as they had no root, they withered when the sun was risen with burning beat. We cannot consider the exhilaration with which hearts receive the novelty of the Gospel to be the very best and surest sign of grace.

Again, we are pleased with children when we see in them much knowledge of the things of God, for in any case such knowledge is most desirable; yet it is not conclusive evidence of conversion. Of course that knowledge may be a divine fruit; if they are taught of the Spirit of God, it is indeed well with them. But as it is more than possible that we ourselves may know the Scriptures and understand the whole theory of the Gospel and yet may not be saved, the like may be true in the case of our youth. The fear of God which is so often neglected is one of the best evidences of sincere piety. We are to work out our own salvation with fear and trembling, for it is God that works in us. When either child or adult has the fear of God before his eyes, this is the finger of God. By this we do not mean the servile fear which works dread and bondage, but that holy fear which pays reverence before the majesty of the Most High and has a high esteem of all things sacred, because God is great and greatly to be praised. Above all things young people need a dread of doing wrong, tenderness of conscience, and anxiety of spirit to please God. Such a principle is a sure work of grace, and a surer proof of the work of the Holy Spirit than all the joy a child can feel or all the knowledge it can acquire. I ask all teachers of the young to look well to this.

There is a growing flightiness about the religion of the present day which makes me tremble. I cannot endure the religion which swims only in boiling water and breathes only in heated air. To me the whisper of the Spirit has no relationship to a brass band; much less does godliness treat the great God and the Holy Savior as matters for irreverent clamor. The deep-seated fear of the Lord is what is wanted, whether in old or young. It is better to tremble at the Word of the Lord and to bow before the infinite majesty of divine love, than to shout oneself hoarse. O that we had more of the stern righteousness of the Puritans or of the inner feeling of the olden Friends. Men nowadays put on their shoes and stamp and kick, and few seem to feel the power of that command, given of old to Moses, "Put off thy shoes from off thy feet, for the place whereon thou standest is holy ground." The truth of God is not meant to inflate us but to humble us before the throne. Obadiah had early piety of the right kind.

Beloved, you do not need that I should at this point speak to you at large upon *the advantages of early piety*. I will, therefore, only sum them up in a few sentences. To be a believer in God early in life is to be saved from a thousand regrets. Such a man shall never have to say that he carries in his bones the sins of his youth. Early piety helps us to form associations for the rest of life which will prove helpful, and it saves us from those which are harmful. The Christian young man will not fall into the common sins of young men and injure his constitution by excesses. He will be likely to be married to a Christian woman and so to have a holy companion in his march toward heaven. He will select as his associates those who will be his friends in the church and not in the tavern, his helpers in virtue and not his tempters to vice. Depend upon it, a great deal depends upon whom we choose for our companions when we begin life. If we start in bad company, it is very hard to break away from it. The man brought to Christ early in life has this further advantage, that he is helped to form holy habits, and he is saved from being the slave of their opposites. Habits soon become a second nature; to form new ones is hard work; but those formed in youth remain in old age. There is something in that verse—

'Tis easier work if we begin
To serve the Lord betimes;
But sinners who grow old in sin
Are hardened in their crimes.

I am sure it is so. Moreover, I notice that, very frequently, those who are brought to Christ while young grow in grace more rapidly and readily than others do. They have not so much to unlearn, and they have not such a heavy weight of old memories to carry. The scars and bleeding sores which come of having spent years in the service of the Devil are missed by those whom the Lord brings into His church before they have wandered far into the world.

As to early piety in its bearing upon others, I cannot too highly commend it. How attractive it is! Grace looks loveliest in youth. That which would not be noticed in the grown-up man strikes at once the most careless observer when seen in a child. Grace in a child has a convincing force; the infidel drops his weapon and admires. A word spoken by a child abides in the memory, and its artless accents touch the heart. Where the minister's sermon fails, the child's prayer may gain the victory. Moreover, religion in children suggests encouragement to those of riper years; for others seeing the little one saved say to themselves, "Why should not we also find the Lord?" By a certain secret power it opens closed doors and turns the key in the lock of unbelief. Where nothing else could win a way for truth, a child's love has done it. It is still true, "Out of the mouth of babes and sucklings hast thou ordained strength because of thine enemies, that thou mightest still the enemy and the avenger." Go on, go on, dear teachers, to promote this most precious of all things beneath the sky, true religion in the heart—especially in the heart of the young.

I have taken up, perhaps, too much time upon this early piety, and therefore I will only give you hints, in the next place, as to its results.

Persevering Piety

Youthful piety leads on to persevering piety. Obadiah could say, "I thy servant fear the Lord from my youth." Time had not changed him; whatever his age may have been, his religion had not decayed. We are all fond of novelty, and I have known some men go wrong as it were for a change. It is not burning quick to the death in martyrdom that is the hard work; roasting before a slow fire is a far more terrible test of firmness. To continue to be gracious during a long life of temptation is to be gracious indeed. For the grace of God to convert a man like Paul, who was full of threatenings against the saints, is a great marvel, but for the grace of God to preserve a believer for ten, twenty, thirty, forty, fifty years is quite as great a miracle and deserves more of our praise than it

112   *Spurgeon's Sermons on Old Testament Men • Book Two*

usually commands. Obadiah was not affected by the lapse of time; he was found to be when old what he was when young.

Nor was he carried away by the fashion of those evil times. To be a servant of Jehovah was thought to be a mean thing, old-fashioned, ignorant, a thing of the past; the worship of Baal was the "modern thought" of the hour. All the court walked after the god of Sidon, and all the courtiers went in the same way. My lord worshiped Baal, and my lady worshiped Baal, for the queen worshiped Baal; but Obadiah said, "I thy servant fear Jehovah from my youth." Blessed is the man who cares nothing for the fashion, for it passes away. If for a while it rages toward evil, what has the believing man to do but to abide steadfastly by the right? Obadiah was not even affected by the absence of the means of grace. The priests and Levites had fled into Judah, and the prophets had been killed or hidden away, and there was no public worship of Jehovah in Israel. The temple was far away at Jerusalem; therefore he had no opportunity of hearing anything that could strengthen him or stimulate him; yet he held on his way. I wonder how long some professors would keep up their profession if there were no places of worship, no Christian associations, no ministrations of the Word; but this man's fear of the Lord was so deep that the absence of that which is usually wanted for the sustenance of piety did not cause him to decline. May you and I personally feed upon the Lord Jesus in the secret of our souls, so that we may flourish even though we should be far removed from a profitable ministry. May the Holy Spirit make us steadfast, unmovable evermore.

Added to this, there were the difficulties of his position. He was chamberlain of the palace. If he had pleased Jezebel and worshiped Baal, he might have been much easier in his situation, for he would have enjoyed her royal patronage; but there he was, governor in Ahab's house and yet fearing Jehovah. He must have had to walk very delicately and watch his words most carefully. I do not wonder that he became a very cautious person and was a little afraid even of Elijah, lest he was giving him a commission which would lead to his destruction. He came to be extremely prudent and looked on things round about so as neither to compromise his conscience nor jeopardize his position. It wants an uncommonly wise man to do that, but he who can accomplish it is to be commended. He did not run away from his position nor retreat from his religion. If he had been forced to do wrong, I am sure he would have imitated the priests and Levites and have fled into Judah, where the worship of Jehovah continued; but he felt that without yielding to idolatry he could do something for God in his advantageous position, and therefore he determined to stop and fight it out.

When there is no hope of victory, you may as well retire; but he is the brave man who when the bugle sounds retreat does not hear it, who puts his blind eye to the telescope and cannot see the signal to cease firing, but just holds his position against all odds and does all the damage he can to the enemy. Obadiah was a man who did in truth "hold the fort," for he felt that when all the prophets were doomed by Jezebel, it was his part to stay near the tigress and save the lives of at least a hundred servants of God from her cruel power. If he could not do more, he would not have lived in vain if he accomplished so much. I admire the man whose decision was equal to his prudence, though I should greatly fear to occupy so perilous a place. His course was something like walking on the tight rope with Blondin. I should not like to try it myself, nor would I recommend any of you to attempt a feat so difficult. The part of Elijah is much safer and grander. The prophet's course was plain enough. He had not to please but to reprove Ahab; he had not to be wary but to act in a bold outspoken manner for the God of Israel. How much the greater man he seems to be when the two stand together in the scene before us. Obadiah falls on his face and calls him "My lord Elijah"; and well he might, for morally he was far his inferior. Yet I must not fall into Elijah's vein myself lest I have to pull myself up with a sharp check. It was a great thing for Obadiah that he could manage Ahab's household with Jezebel in it, and yet, for all that, win this commendation from the Spirit of God, that *he feared the Lord greatly.*

He persevered, too, notwithstanding his success in life; and that I hold to be much to his credit. There is nothing more perilous to a man than to prosper in this world and become rich and respectable. Of course we desire it, wish for it, strive for it; but how many in winning it have lost all, as to spiritual wealth! The man used to love the people of God, and now he says, "They are a vulgar class of persons." So long as he could hear the Gospel, he did not mind the architecture of the house; but now he has grown aesthetic and must have a spire, gothic architecture, a marble pulpit, priestly millinery, a conservatory in the church, and all sorts of pretty things. As he has filled his pocket he has emptied his brains, and especially emptied his heart. He has gotten away from truth and principle in proportion as he has made an advance in his estate. This is a mean business, which at one time he would have been the first to condemn. There is no chivalry in such conduct; it is dastardly to the last degree. God save us from it; but a great many people are not saved from it. Their religion is not a matter of principle, but a matter of interest. It is not the pursuit of truth, but a hankering after society, whatever that may mean. It is not their object to glorify God, but to get rich husbands for their girls. It is not conscience that guides them, but the hope of being able to invite Sir John to dinner with them and of dining at the hall in return. Do not think I am sarcastic. I speak in sober sadness of things which make one feel ashamed. I hear of them daily, though they do not personally affect me or this church. This is an age of meannesses disguised under the notion of respectability. God send us men of the stuff of John Knox or, if you prefer it, of the adamantine metal of Elijah; and if these should prove too stiff and stern, we could even be content with such men as Obadiah. Possibly these last might be harder to produce than Elijahs—with God all things are possible.

Eminent Piety

Obadiah with his early grace and persevering decision became a man of eminent piety, and this is the more remarkable considering what he was and where he was. Eminent piety in a Lord High Chamberlain of Ahab's court! This is a wonder of grace indeed. This man's religion was intense within him. If he did not make the open use of it that Elijah did, he was not called to such a career; but it dwelt deep within his soul and others knew it. Jezebel knew it, I have no doubt whatever. She did not like him, but she had to endure him; she looked askance at him, but she could not dislodge him. Ahab had learned to trust him and could not do without him, for he probably furnished him with a little strength of mind. Possibly Ahab liked to retain him just to show Jezebel that he could be obstinate if he liked and was still a man. I have noticed that the most yielding husbands like to indulge in some notion that they are not quite governed by their spouses, and it is possible that on this account Ahab retained Obadiah in his position. At any rate, there he was, and he never yielded to Ahab's sin nor countenanced his idolatry. Account for it how you may, it is a singular circumstance that in the center of rebellion against God there was one whose devotion to God was intense and distinguished. As it is horrible to find a Judas among the apostles, so it is grand to discover an Obadiah among Ahab's courtiers. What grace must have been at work to maintain such a fire in the midst of the sea, such godliness in the midst of the vilest iniquity!

And his eminent piety was very *practical*; for when Jezebel was slaying the prophets, he hid them away from her—one hundred of them. I do not know how many servants of the Lord any of you support, but I have not the privilege of knowing any gentleman who sustains a hundred ministers; this man's hospitality was on a grand scale. He fed them with the best he could find for them and risked his life for them by hiding them away in caves from the search of the queen. He not only used his purse but staked his life when a price was set upon these men's heads. How many among us would place our lives in jeopardy for one of the Lord's servants? At any rate, Obadiah's fear of the Lord brought forth precious fruit and proved itself to be a powerful principle of action.

His godliness was such, too, that it was recognized by the believers of the day. I feel sure of that, because Obadiah said to Elijah, "Was it not told my lord how I hid the Lord's prophets?" Now, Elijah was the well-known head and leader of the followers of Jehovah throughout that whole nation, and Obadiah was a little astonished that somebody had not told the great prophet about his deed; so that though his generous act may have been concealed from Jezebel and the Baalites, it was well known among the servants of the living God. He was well reported of among those whose good report is worth having; it was whispered about among them that they had a friend at court, that the chamberlain of the palace was on their side. If anybody could rescue a prophet, he could, and therefore the prophets of God felt secure in giving themselves up to his care; they knew that he would not betray them to bloodthirsty Jezebel. Their coming to him and confiding in him shows that his faithfulness was well known and highly esteemed. Thus he was strong enough in grace to be a leader recognized by the godly party.

He himself evidently knew Elijah and did not disdain at once to pay him the utmost reverence. The prophet of God, who was at that moment hated of all men because of the judgment which had been inflicted by his means and was the special object of the king's pursuit, was honored by this gracious man. Early piety is likely to become eminent piety; the man who is likely to fear God greatly is the man who serves God early. You know the old proverb, "He that would thrive must rise at five." It is as applicable to religion as to anything else. He that would thrive with God must be with God early in his days. He who would make great progress in the heavenward race must not lose a moment. Let me urge young people to think of this and give their hearts to God even now.

Sunday school teachers, you may be training today the men who will keep the truth alive in this land in years to come, the men who will take care of God's servants and be their best allies, the men and women who will win souls to Christ. Go you on with your holy work. You do not know whom you have about you. You might well imitate the tutor who took his hat off to the boys in his school because he did not know what they would turn out to be. Think very highly of your class. You cannot tell who may be there; but assuredly you may have among them those who shall be pillars in the house of God in years to come.

Comfortable Piety

Obadiah's early religion became comfortable piety to him afterward. When he thought Elijah was about to expose him to great danger, he pleaded his long service of God, saying, "I thy servant fear the Lord from my youth"; just as David, when he grew old, said, "O God, thou hast taught me from my youth: and hitherto have I declared thy wondrous works; now also when I am old and grayheaded, O God, forsake me not." It will be a great comfort to you, young people, when you grow old to look back upon a life spent in the service of God. You will not trust in it; you will not think that there is any merit in it; but you will bless God for it. A servant who has been with his master from his youth ought not to be turned adrift when he grows gray. A right-minded master respects the person who has served him long and well. Suppose you had living in the family an old nurse who had nursed you when you were a child and had lived to bring up your children, would you turn her into the street when she was past her work? No; you will do your best for her; if it is in your power, you will keep her out of the workhouse. Now, the Lord is much more kind and gracious than we are, and He will never turn off His old servants, I sometimes cry—

> Dismiss me not thy service, Lord,
>   But train me for thy will;
> For even I, in fields so broad,
>   Some duties may fulfill;
> And I will ask for no reward,
>   Except to serve thee still.

I anticipate the time when I shall not be able to do all I do now. You and I may look forward a little to the nearing period when we shall pass from middle life to declining years, and we may be assured that our Lord will take care of us to the last. Let us do our diligence to serve Him while we have health and strength, and we may be sure that He is not unrighteous to forget our work of faith and labor of love. It is not the way of Him. "Having loved his own which were in the world he loved them to the end." That was said of His Son, and it may be said of the Father also. Oh, believe me, there is no better crutch on which an old man can lean than the fact of God's love to him when he was young. You cannot have a better outlook to your window when your eyes begin to fail then to remember how you went after the Lord in the days of your youth and devoted your vigor to his service.

Dear young people, if any of you are living in sin, I do pray you to recollect that if you are seeking the pleasures of this world today, you will have to pay for it by-and-by. Rejoice in your youth, and let your heart cheer you therein; but for all this the Lord will bring you into judgment. If your childhood be vanity and your youth be wickedness, your after-days will be sorrow. Oh, that you would be wise and offer to Christ your flower in its bud with all its beauty upon it. You cannot be too soon holy, for you cannot be too soon happy. A truly merry life must begin in the Great Father's house.

And you, teachers, go on teaching the young the ways of God. In these days the State is giving them secular instruction all the day long, six days in the week; and religious teaching is greatly needed to balance it, or we shall soon become a nation of infidels. Secular teaching is all very well and good; we never stand in the way of any sort of light. But teaching that has not religion blended with it will simply help men to be bigger rascals than they would be without it. A rogue with a jemmy is bad enough, but a rogue with a pen and a set of cooked accounts robs a hundred for the other's one. Under our present plans children will grow up with greater capacity for mischief, unless the fear of the Lord is set before them, and they are taught in the Scriptures and the Gospel of our Lord Jesus. Instead of relaxing Sunday school efforts, we shall be wise to increase them greatly.

As to you that have grown old in sin, I cannot talk to you about early piety; but there is a passage of Scripture which ought to give you great hope. Remember how the householder went out at the third, the sixth, the ninth, and at last at the eleventh hour and found some still standing in the marketplace idle. It was late, was it not? Very late. But, blessed be God, it was not too late. They had but one hour left, but the master said, "Go, work in my vineyard, and whatsoever is right I will give thee." Now you eleventh-hour people, you people of sixty, sixty-five, seventy, seventy-five, eighty—I would go on to one hundred if I thought you were here of that age—you still may come and enlist in the service of the gracious Lord, who will give you your penny at the close of the day even as He will give to the rest of the laborers. The Lord bring you to His feet by faith in Christ. Amen.

9

A Lesson from the Life of King Asa

Herein thou hast done foolishly: therefore from henceforth thou shalt have wars (2 Chronicles 16:9).

O ur text leads us to speak upon historical matters, and for this I shall by no means apologize, although I have sometimes heard very foolish professors speak slightingly of the historical part of Scripture. Remember that the historical books were almost the only Scripture possessed by the early saints; and from those they learned the mind of God. David sang the blessedness of the man who delighted in the law of the Lord, yet he had only the first five books and, perhaps, Joshua, Judges, and Ruth, all books of history, in which to meditate day and night. The psalmist himself spoke most lovingly of these books, which were the only statutes and testimonies of the Lord to him, with, perhaps, the addition of the Book of Job. Other saints delighted in the histories of the word before the more spiritual books came in their way at all. If rightly viewed, the histories of the Old Testament are full of instruction. They supply us both with warnings and examples in the realm of practical morals; and hidden within their letter, like pearls in oyster shells, lie grand spiritual truths couched in allegory and metaphor. I may say of the least important of all the books what our Lord said of children, "Take heed that ye despise not one of these little ones." To take away from Holy Writ involves a curse upon the daring deed—may we never incur the penalty! All Scripture is given by inspiration and is profitable; be it ours to gain the profit. Let us see whether we cannot get a lesson from the life of King Asa.

This sermon was taken from *The Metropolitan Tabernacle Pulpit* and was preached at the Metropolitan Tabernacle, Newington, in 1874.

Who Asa Was and What He Had Done in His Better Days

We will commence by noticing who he was and what he had done in his better days, for this will help to understand more clearly the fault into which he fell. He was a man of whom it is said that his heart was perfect before God all his days. It is a great thing to have said of anyone; indeed, it is the greatest commendation which can be pronounced upon mortal man. When the heart, the intention, the master-affection is right, the man is reckoned a good man before the Lord, notwithstanding that there may be a thousand things which are not commendable—yes, and some things which are censurable in the man's outward career. Asa is noticeable in the early part of his life for the fact that he set up the worship of God and carried it out with great diligence, though his mother was an idolater and his father, Abijah, was little better. He had enjoyed no training as a youth that could lead him aright, but quite the contrary. Yet he was very decided, even in the first days of his reign, for the Lord his God and acted in all things with an earnest desire to glorify Jehovah and to lead his people away from all idols to the worship of the true God. Now, a life may begin well and yet may be clouded before its close; the verdure of earnestness may fade into the sere and yellow leaf of backsliding. We may have the grace of God in our earliest days, but unless we have day by day fresh help from on high, dead flies may pollute the ointment and spoil the sweet odor of our lives. We shall need to watch against temptation so long as we are in this wilderness of sin. Only in heaven are we out of gunshot of the Devil. Though we may have been kept in the ways of the Lord, as Asa was for fifty or sixty years, yet if left by the Master for a single moment, we shall bring discredit upon His holy name.

In the middle of his reign Asa was put to the test by a very serious trial. He was attacked by the Ethiopians, and they came against him in mighty swarms. What a host to be arrayed against poor little Judah—an army of a million footmen and three hundred thousand chariots! All the host that Asa could muster—and he did his best—was but small compared to this mighty band; and it appeared as if the whole land would be eaten up, for the people seemed sufficient to carry away Judea by handfuls. But Asa believed in God, and therefore when he had mustered his little band, he committed the battle to the Lord his God. Read attentively that earnest believing prayer which he offered. "And Asa cried unto the Lord his God, and said, Lord, it is nothing with thee to help, whether with many, or with them that have no power: help us, O Lord our God; for we rest on thee, and in thy name we go against this multitude. O Lord, thou art our God; let not man prevail against thee." How grandly he threw all his burden upon God! He declared that he rested in the Most High and believed that God could as well achieve the victory by a few and feeble folk as by a vast army; after this prayer he marched to the battle with holy confidence, and God gave him the victory. The power of Ethiopia was broken before him, and Judah's armies returned laden with the spoil. You would not have thought that a man who could perform that grand action would become, a little after, full of unbelief; but the greatest faith of yesterday will not give us confidence for today unless the fresh springs which are in God shall overflow again. Even Abraham, who at one time staggered not at the promise through unbelief, yet did stagger some time afterward about a far less difficult matter. The greatest of God's servants, if their Lord hides His face, soon sink even below the least; all the strength of the strongest lies in Him.

After Asa had thus by divine strength won a great victory, he did not, as some do, grow proud of it, but he set to work, in obedience to a prophetic warning, to purge his country by a thorough reformation. He did it and did it well. He did not show any partiality toward the rich and great in his country who were guilty of the worship of false gods, for the queen-mother was a great fosterer of idolatry, and she had a grove of her own with a temple in it, in which was her own peculiar idol. But the king put her away from her eminent position, took her idol and not merely broke it but stamped upon it and burned it with every sign of contempt at the brook Kidron into which ran the sewage of the temple, to let the people know that, whether in high places or among the poor, there should be nothing left to provoke the Lord throughout the land. This was well done.

Oh that such a reformation might happen in this land, for the country is beginning to be covered with idols and mass-houses! Everywhere they are setting up the altars of their breaden deity, shrines to the queen of heaven, the crucifix and the saints, while the spiritual worship of God is put aside to make room for vain shows and spiritual masquerades. The God of the Reformation—how much is He forgotten nowadays! Oh for a return of the days of Knox and his covenanting brethren! Asa was for a root and branch reform, and he went through with it bravely. You would not have thought that a man so thorough—a man who, like Levi of old, knew not his own mother when it came to the matter of serving God, but made "through stitch" with it, as the old writers used to say—you would not have supposed that he would be the man who, when he came into another trial, would be running after an idolater and cringing before him and praying him to give him his help. Alas, the best of men are men at the best! God alone is unchangeable. He alone is good always, or indeed at all. "There is none good save one, that is God." We are only good as He makes us good; and if His hand be withdrawn even for a moment, we start aside like a deceitful bow or a broken bone which has been badly set. Alas, how soon are the mighty fallen and the weapons of war broken, if the Lord uphold not! Asa, who could do marvels and who walked so well and thoroughly before his God, yet nevertheless came to do foolishly and bring upon himself lifelong chastisement.

I have thus brought before you his character, because it was most fitting to start with this; it was due to his memory and due to ourselves; for we must remember that whatever we shall have to say against him, he was assuredly a child of God. His heart was right; he was a sincere, genuine, gracious believer. If any object that he had grievous faults and therefore could not be a child of God, I shall be obliged to answer that they must first of all produce a faultless child of God this side of heaven before they will have sufficient ground for such an objection. I find that the holiest of men in Scripture had their imperfections, with the sole exception of our Master, the Apostle and High Priest of our profession, in whom was no sin. His garments were whiter than any fuller could make them, but all His servants had their spots. He is light, and in Him is no darkness at all, but we, with all the brightness His grace has given us, are poor dim lamps at best. I make no exception even of those who claim perfection, for I have no more faith in their perfection than in the Pope's infallibility. There is enough of the earthen vessel left about the best of the Lord's servants to show that they are earthen and that the excellency of the heavenly treasure of divine grace which is put within them may be clearly seen to be of God and not of them.

The Grave Error into Which Asa Fell

Now, we shall turn to notice the foolishness for which the prophet rebuked him. He was threatened by Baasha, the king of the neighboring territory of Israel. He was not directly assailed by war, but Baasha began to build a fortress which would command the passages between the two countries and prevent the people of Israel from coming to settle in the land of Judah or make their annual pilgrimages to Jerusalem. Now, one would naturally have expected, from Asa's former conduct, that he would either have thought very little of Baasha or else that he would have taken the case before God, as he did before in the matter of the Ethiopians. But this was a smaller trouble altogether, and somehow, I fancy, it was because it was a smaller trouble Asa thought that he could manage it very well himself by the help of an arm of flesh. In the case of the invasion by countless hordes of Ethiopians, Asa must have felt that it was of no use calling in Ben-hadad, the king of Syria, or asking any of the nations to help him, for with all their help he would not have been equal to the tremendous struggle. Therefore he was driven to God. But this being a smaller trial, he does not seem to have been so thoroughly divorced from confidence in man. But he looked about him, and thought that Ben-hadad, the heathen king of Syria, might be led to attack the king of Israel and so draw him away from building the new fort, divide his attention, cripple his resources, and give Judah a fine opportunity of attacking him. Believers frequently behave worse in little trials than in great ones. I have known some children of God who have borne with equanimity the loss of almost everything they had, who have been disturbed and distracted and led into all sorts of doubt and mistrust by troubles that were scarcely worth the mentioning. How is it that vessels which bear a hurricane may, nevertheless, be driven upon a sand bank when there is but a capful of wind—that ships which have navigated the broad ocean have yet foundered in a narrow stream? It only proves this, that it is not the severity of the trial, it is the having or not having of God's presence that is the main thing; for in the great trial with the Ethiopians God's grace gave Asa faith, but in the little trial about Baasha, king of Israel, Asa had no faith and began to look about him for help from men.

Observe that Asa went off to Ben-hadad, the king of Syria, who was a worshiper of a false god, with whom he ought to have had no connection or alliance whatever; and, what was worse, he induced Ben-hadad to break his league with Baasha. Here was a child of God teaching the ungodly to be untrue—a man of God becoming an instructor for Satan, teaching a heathen to be false to his promise. This was policy. This is the kind of thing which the kings of the earth practice toward one another; they are always ready to break treaties, though bound by the most solemn pledges. They make but light of covenant. The great matter with ambassadors even nowadays is to see which can entangle the other, for, as a statesman once said, "An ambassador is a person who is sent abroad to lie for the good of his country." Oh, the tricks, plots, deceptions, equivocations, and intrigues of diplomacy! No chapter in human history shows up our fallen nature in more mournful colors. Asa, I have no doubt, thought that all was fair in war. He took the common rule, the common standard of mankind, and went upon that, whereas, as a child of God, he ought to have scorned anything that was dishonorable or untrue. As to saying to a heathen king, "Break thy league with Baasha, and make a league with me"—why, if he had been in a right state of heart, he would sooner have lost his tongue than have uttered such disgraceful words.

But, child of God as he was, when he once got off the plain simple way of believing in God and taking his trouble to God, there was no telling what he would do. When you set the helm of your vessel toward the point to which you mean to steer and steer right on whatever comes in your way, then your course will be well enough if you have a motive power within independent of wind and tide. But when you take to tacking this way, then you will have in due time to tack the other way; and when policy makes you do this wrong thing, policy will lead you to do another wrong thing, and so on, to a most lamentable degree. When our walk is with the Lord, it is a safe, holy, honorable walk, but the way of the flesh is evil and ends in shame. If you follow the way of the world, though always a crowded way, it will turn out before long to be a miserable, pettifogging, cringing, humiliating, wretched way, dishonorable to the true-born heir of heaven. Dust shall be the serpent's meat, and if we practice the crawling, twisting, slimy arts of the serpent, we shall have to eat the dust too. Should a child of God degrade himself in that fashion? If he acts as he should act, he acts like a nobleman, no, like a prince of the blood imperial of heaven, for is he not a son of God, one of heaven's true aristocracy? But when he degenerates to acting as worldlings do, then, alas! he stains his garments in the mire.

I charge you, my dear brethren and sisters, to look well to this. Perhaps I may be speaking as God's mouth to some of you who are now entering upon a testing time, a trouble in the family, a trial in business, or a difficulty in reference to a contemplated marriage, and you are asking, "What course shall I take?" You know what a man of the world would do, and it has been suggested to you that such a course is the right one for you to follow. My dear brother, remember you are not of the world, even as Christ is not of the world; mind you act accordingly. If you are a worldly man and do as worldly men do, why I must leave you, for them that are without God judgeth; but if you are a man of God and an heir of heaven, I beseech you, do not follow custom, or do a wrong thing because others would do it, or do a little evil for the sake of a great good, but in your confidence possess your soul, and abide faithful to conscience and to the eternal law of rectitude. Let others do as they please, but as for you, set the Lord always before you, and let integrity and uprightness preserve you. Ask the Lord to help you. Is it not written that He will with the temptation make a way of escape? "Cast thy burden upon the Lord: he will sustain thee. He will never suffer the righteous to be moved." Do not put forth your hand to iniquity. You may, in order to help yourself, do in five minutes what you cannot undo in fifty years. You may bring upon yourself a lifelong series of trial by one single unbelieving action. Beware of staying yourself on Egypt and sending for help to Assyria, for these will distress you but help you not. Cry, "Lord, increase our faith!" That is what you greatly need in the trying hour, lest you should, like Asa, first of all turn from confidence in God, and then, looking to an arm of flesh, should be tempted to use illegitimate means in order to induce the creature to let you rely upon it.

Asa, having advanced so far in the wrong path, did worse still, if worse could be; for he took of the gold and silver which belonged to the house of the Lord, in order to purchase therewith the alliance of the Syrian monarch. I will say nothing about what belonged to his own house. He might do as he liked with that so long as he did not spend it upon sin, but he took of the treasure that belonged to the house of the Lord and gave it to Ben-hadad to bribe him to break his league with Baasha and be in league with himself. Thus God was robbed that the unbelieving king might find help in an arm of flesh. And, "Will a man rob God?" Yet a Christian never doubts God, and looks to the creature, without robbing Him. If you rob Him of nothing else, you rob Him of His honor. Shall a father find his child trusting a stranger rather than his own sire? Shall the husband see his wife putting confidence in his enemy? Will not that rob him of that which is far more precious than gold? Is it not a breach of that undivided affection and that complete confidence which ought to exist in the conjugal relationship? And shall I mistrust my heavenly Father, my Almighty Helper, and put confidence in a poor, broken reed? Shall I cast my burden upon a poor fellow sinner and forget to rest in my Savior? Shall the Well-beloved of my soul be only trusted in fair weather? And shall I have such a sorry opinion of Him that, when it comes to a little storm, I run to someone else and ask him to be my refuge? Beloved, let it not be so with us, or we shall surely grieve the Lord and bring ourselves into much perplexity. Have we not been guilty of this enough already? Shall we provoke the Lord to jealousy? Are we bent upon grieving His Holy Spirit? Can we not take warning from Asa? Need we run upon this rock when we can see the wrecks of others all around? The Lord grant we may take heed, according to His Word!

So this good man, by his want of faith, fell into many sins. For I am compelled to add that he had to bear the blame of the consequences of his conduct. When Ben-hadad, the king of Syria, came up and attacked Israel, he did not content himself with a battle or two, but he fell to plundering the Israelites and murdering them by wholesale, so that great sorrows were brought upon the people of Israel. And who was to blame for these sorrows but the king of Judah, who had hired the Syrians for that very purpose? He who ought to have been a brother to the Israelites became their destroyer, and every time the cruel sword of the Syrians slew the women and children of Israel, the poor afflicted people had Asa to thank for it. The beginning of sin is like the letting out of waters; none can foresee what devastation the floods may cause. Brethren, we can never tell what may be the consequences of one wrong action; we may kindle a fire in the forest merely to warm our own hands, but where the sparks may fly and how many leagues the conflagration may spread, an angel cannot prophesy. Let us jealously keep away from every doubtful deed, lest we bring evil consequences upon others as well as ourselves. If we carry no matches, we shall cause no explosions. Oh, for a holy jealousy, a deep conscientiousness and, above all, a solemn conscientiousness on the point of faith! To rest in the Lord—that is our business; to stay ourselves only upon Him—that is our sole concern. "My soul, wait thou only upon God, for my expectation is from him." Unbelief is in itself idolatry; unbelief leads us to look to the creature, which is folly; and to look to the creature is, in effect, to worship the creature, to put it into God's place, and so to grieve God and set up a rival in the holy place.

I want you to listen yet a little while longer to this story of Asa. It came to pass that Asa's hiring Ben-hadad turned out to be a fine thing for him, and, in the judgment of everybody who looked on, I dare say it was said that it was a fortunate stroke of business. According to God's mind, the king's course was evil, but it did not turn out badly for him politically. Now, many people in the world judge actions by their immediate results. If a Christian does a wrong thing and it prospers, then at once they conclude he was justified in doing it; but, ah! brethren, this is a poor, blind way of judging the actions of men and the providence of God. Do you not know that there are Devil's providences as well as God's providences? I mean this. Jonah wanted to go to Tarshish to flee from God, and he went down to Joppa; and what? Why, he found a ship just going to Tarshish. What a providence! What a providence! Are you so foolish as to view it in that light? I do not think Jonah was of that mind when he cried to God out of the deeps. When the chief priests and Pharisees would take Jesus, they found Judas ready to betray him. Was this also a providence? May not Satan have some hand in the arrangement which lays a weapon so near a murderer's hand or renders robbery and fraud so easy? Do you think it an instance of divine goodness that the tares often grow plentifully when the wheat suffers from drought. Often have we observed people who wanted to do wrong, and things have just happened rightly to help them; and they have therefore said, "What a providence!" Ah, but a providence that was meant to test and try, not a providence that was intended to aid and abet in the doing of a wrong thing. A providence not to rejoice in, but concerning which we are taught to pray, "Lead us not into temptation, but deliver us from evil." A wrong is a wrong, whatever comes of it. If by uttering one falsehood you could become a rich man forever, it would not change the nature of the falsehood. If by doing one wrong transaction you could rid yourself from all liabilities in business and be henceforth in competent circumstances, that would not, before God, take off the edge of the evil, no, not a single jot. God was pleased, for wise reasons, to allow the policy of his erring servant Asa to prosper, but now you will see that Asa was put in a worse place than ever because of it.

The trial of Asa's spirit, the testing of his unswerving faithfulness, whether he would walk before God or not, became more severe than before, for God sent His servant the prophet to him, and he said to him, "When you came to God, and trusted him about the Ethiopians, did not God prosper you? Though there were so many of them, did not the Lord give you the victory? And now you have gone away from your faith, you have lost a great blessing by it; for if you had trusted in God, you would have gone to war against Baasha and Ben-hadad, and you would have beaten them both, and your own kingdom would have grown strong by the putting down of these rival kingdoms. But you have lost that; you have acted very foolishly, and God means to chasten you for it, for from this very day you will have no more peace, but you will have war so long as you are a king." Now, observe, if king Asa had met with a trouble when he acted unjustifiably, he would have been humble, I have no doubt. Then he would have seen how wrong he was, and he would have repented; but inasmuch as what he had done did not bring disaster with it, and God did not chasten him, the king's heart grew proud, and he said, "Who is this fellow that he should come to tell his king his duty? Does he think I do not know, as well as he can tell me, what is right and what is wrong? Put the arrogant intruder in prison."

When a prophet came to Rehoboam, who was a bad king, Rehoboam did not put him in prison; he respected and reverenced the word of the Lord. A bad man may do better than a good man on some one particular occasion; and so Rehoboam did better in that matter than Asa did. But Asa was now all wrong; he was in a high hectoring spirit; and this was but what we might have expected, for whenever a man will cringe before his fellowmen, you may be sure he is beginning to walk proudly before God. In his haughtiness of heart he put the prophet in prison. Instead of weeping and humbling himself for what he had done, he imprisoned his reprover; and then, being in an irritable temper and a domineering humor, he began to oppress certain of his people. I do not know who they may have been, but probably they were godly persons who sympathized with the prophet and said, "We shall surely meet with a terrible judgment for dealing thus with God's servant." Perhaps they spoke freely about it, and so he put them in prison too. Thus God's own child had become the persecutor of God's servant and of other faithful ones. Oh, it was very sad, very sad! Well might God then resolve that the angry should smart for his faults very severely, that the rod should come home to his bone and his flesh and render his remaining days exceeding sorrowful.

O beloved friends, among your most earnest prayers pray God never to let your sins prosper; for if they do, they will breed a gangrene in your spirit which will lead on to yet more dangerous diseases of soul and will inevitably entail upon you a dreary inheritance of affliction. God does not always whip His children the next minute after they do wrong. Sometimes He tells them that the rod will come and so makes them smart in apprehension before they smart in actual experience, for they are thinking of what it will be, and that may be even a worse trial to them than the trial itself. But as surely as they are His own peculiar people, they must and shall be taught that sin is an exceeding great evil, and they shall have no joy of their dalliance with it.

Thus I have shown you who Asa was and what faults he fell into and how this led to other faults; and now we have to show you *what God did with him when he came to a close reckoning.* "Now," He seemed to say, "I will take you in hand Myself," and He sent him a disease in his feet—a very painful disease too. He had to suffer night and day; he was tormented with it and found no rest. God's own hand was heavy upon him. Some of us know to our cost that disease in the feet can become a very grievous affliction, second indeed to none, unless it be a malady of the brain. Now did the king learn that embroidered slippers give no ease to gouty feet and that sleep flies when disease bears rule. This should have driven Asa to repentance, but, to show that afflictions of themselves will not set a man right, Asa had fallen into such an unbelieving spirit that instead of sending to God for help and crying for relief to Him who sent the disease, he sent for the physicians. It is not wrong to send for physicians; it is quite right; but it is very wrong to send for physicians in place of crying to God, thus putting the human agency before the divine; besides, it is very probable that these physicians were only heathenish conjurers, necromancers, and pretenders to magical arts and could not be consulted without implicating the patient in their evil practices. Though Asa would not approve of their heathenism, yet he might think, "Well, they are famous for their cures, and who they may be is not so much my concern. I will put up with that; if they can cure me, they may come." So his unbelief deprived him of the cure which God could readily enough have given him, and he had his physicians and their physic, but they were miserable comforters to him, giving him no relief and probably causing him to suffer more than he would have suffered without them. They were physicians of no value, and their medicines were a delusion. How often is it so when we persist in looking away from God. He who has God has all, but he who has all besides God has really nothing at all.

Asa's life after that period was a life of war and pain. His evening was clouded, and his sun set in tempest. Have you never noticed the career of David? What a happy life David's was up to one point! In his youth he was hunted like a partridge upon the mountains, but he was very merry. What joyful psalms he used to sing when he was a humble shepherd boy! And when afterward he was an exile in the caves of Engedi, how gloriously he poured out notes of gratitude and joy! He was at that period, and for years after, one of the happiest of men. But that hour when he walked on the roof of his house and saw Bathsheba and gave way to his unholy desires put an end to the happy days of David; and though he was a child of God and God never cast him away, yet his heavenly Father never ceased to chasten him. From that day his life teems with trouble—troubles from his own children one after another, ingratitude from his subjects, and annoyance from his enemies. Afflictions sprang up for him as plenteously as hemlock in the furrows. He became a weeping monarch instead of a rejoicing one. The whole tenor of his life is changed; a somber shade is cast over his entire image. You recognize him as the same man, but his voice is broken; his music is deep bass; he cannot reach the high notes of the scale. From the hour in which he sinned he began to sorrow more and more.

So will it be with us if we are not watchful. We may have led very happy lives in Christ up to this moment, and we know the Lord will not cast us away, for He does not cast away His people whom He did foreknow. But if we begin to walk distrustfully and adopt wrong actions and dishonor His name, He may from this moment say, "You only have I known of all the people of the earth, therefore I will punish you for your iniquities. Because I love you I will chasten you, for I chasten every son whom I love. And now, because you have thus gone astray, you shall be filled with your own backslidings. Your own vanities shall become your vexation throughout the rest of your days." Asa does not appear to have had any peace until at last he fell asleep, and then, I trust, his dying bed was as sweetly perfumed with penitence and pardon as his funeral couch was odoriferous with fragrant spices. The sweet spices of forgiving love and reviving faith were there, and he died rejoicing in his God through the great sacrifice brought back after a time of wandering, the cloudy day at last ending in a calm, bright evening. But who wishes to go so far astray, even if he be at length restored? O brethren, we do not merely want to go to heaven, but we desire to enjoy a heaven on the road to heaven. We would like not only to come up from the wilderness, but to come up from the wilderness leaning on our Beloved. We would not wish to be saved "so as by fire," but to have an abundant entrance administered to us into the kingdom of our Lord and Savior Jesus Christ.

Asa's character was well known among the people, and they loved and respected him. The mistake he had made grieved many of the godly, I do not doubt; but for all that, they felt that one fault must not blot out the recollection of nearly forty years of devoted service to God. So they loved him and they honored him with a funeral worthy of a king, a funeral by which they expressed both their sorrow and their esteem. But may it never be said of you and of me, "He led a good life. He was eminent in the service of God and did much; but there was an unhappy day in which the weakness of the flesh mastered the inner life." O dear sister, if you have brought up your children and have seen your family about you, and they have been proofs to all the world of the way in which you have walked with God and of your care to discharge your duties, do not let your old age be given up to petulance and murmuring and complaining, so that your friends will have to say of you, "At the last she was not the happy Christian woman that she used to be." My dear brother, you have been a merchant, and you have resisted a great many temptations, and you have been noted for your honorable character, do not now in a moment of extreme trial begin to doubt your God. May the Holy Spirit preserve you from so great an ill. In the time of your need you will find the Lord to be Jehovah-jireh. He is no fair-weather friend, but He is a shelter from the storm, a covert from the tempest. Stand fast in your faith in Him. Do not question your God and do questionable things in consequence, for, if you do, it will be said by those who come after you and perhaps even while you live by those who love you, "He was a good man, but there was a sad period of weakness and inconsistency, and though he was deeply penitent, yet from that unhappy day he went limping to his tomb."

What a precious Christ we have, who saves such sinners as we are at all! What a dear and blessed Lord we have, who does not cast us away, notwithstanding all our slips and falls and shameful wanderings. Beloved, let us not be so base as wantonly to grieve Him—

> We have no fear that thou shouldst lose
> One whom eternal love could choose;
> But we would ne'er this grace abuse
> Let us not fall. Let us not fall.

With such a warning as this of Asa before us now, do not let us relax our watchfulness and insensibly turn aside. "The path of the just is as the shining light, which shineth more and more unto the perfect day." That is your model; that is the promise which Scripture sets before you. Plead it, and try to realize it. Let us go from strength to strength. Let us ask to grow in grace and in the knowledge of our Lord and Savior Jesus Christ. If we have wanted props hitherto—outward and visible props— and have not been able altogether to rely upon God, may the Lord help us to grow stronger, so that we may have done with Ready-to-Halt's crutches. May we walk uprightly before the Lord because we rely upon Him, trusting ever in His sure faithfulness and in the power which guarantees that His promise shall be fulfilled.

I do not know to whom I may be speaking a needful word, except that I know it is needful for myself. Perhaps there are some here to whom it may be just the word that is wanted. Dear brother, the life of faith is a blessed one. A believer's course is a tried one; it is a warfare; but, for all that, all the sorrows of faith put together do not equal in bitterness one drop of the sorrow of sin or one grain of the misery of unbelief. The king's highway may be rough, but By-path Meadow in the long run is the rougher way of the two. It looks very pleasant to walk on the green turf, but, remember, it is only in appearance that By-path Meadow is smooth. The ways of Christ are ways of pleasantness. All His paths are peace, as compared with any other paths in the world; and if they were not—if to serve the Lord led us only into sorrow and trouble—I trust the loyal hearts here, the virgin souls whom Christ has chosen, would resolve through floors or flames, if Jesus led the way, to follow still. O beloved, may you cleave to the Lord by a simple faith! May you cleave to Him when the many turn aside! May you witness that He has the living Word, and none upon earth beside! Because your hearts are frail and feeble, ask Him now to cast the bands of His love about you, and the cords of a man, to bind you fast to His altar, that you may not go away from it; for except He hold you fast, you must—you will—decline and prove apostates after all. But He will hold you; He will keep the feet of His saints. Only trust not in yourselves. "He that trusteth in his own heart is a fool." If any man say, "I stand," let him take heed lest he fall. Beware of that self-confidence and spiritual boasting which is becoming common among Christians, aye, and among some of the better sort, who can even brag of their attainments; when, if they did but know themselves, they would confess that they are nothing better, even at the best, than poor, naked, miserable sinners and have need to look to Jesus, for they are nothing but empty boasters apart from Him, since only in Christ are we anything. "When I am weak, then am I strong," but at no other time. When I think I have whereof to glory, then am I indeed despicable; I know not myself and am become purblind, so as only to see what my own pride makes me think I see. May the Holy Spirit keep us humble—keep us at the foot of the cross—keep us flat on the promise, resting on the eternal rock, and crying, "Nothing am I, Lord—nothing; but You are all in all. I am all emptiness; come and fill me. I am all nakedness; come and clothe me. I am all weakness; come and glorify Your power by making use of me!"

God bless you, dear friends, and if there be any among you who have not a God to trust in or a Savior to love, may you seek Jesus now! If you seek Him, He will be found of you; for whosoever believes in Him is saved, whosoever trusts Christ is saved. Pardon and salvation belong to every soul that hangs its hope upon the Cross. May God bless you richly, for Christ's sake. Amen.

10

Jotham's Peculiar Honor

So Jotham became mighty, because he prepared his ways before the Lord *his God (2 Chronicles 27:6).*

This is a very singular expression which is used here concerning Jotham, who is one of the kings of Judah who are commended as having done that which was right in the sight of the Lord. All of them had their faults, yet they were the best monarchs that sat upon the throne of Judah; and concerning Jotham it is mentioned as his peculiar honor that he "became mighty, because, he prepared his ways before the Lord his God."

I want to draw your attention to this ancient king and specially to point out to you, first, *the peculiar circumstances of Jotham's life*; secondly, *the peculiar distinction of his character*; and then, thirdly, *the peculiar honor of his career*. He "became mighty, because he prepared his ways before the Lord his God."

The Peculiar Circumstances of Jotham's Life

And, to begin with, *he was the son of a good father*, and I should suppose, from the mention of his mother here, of a good mother too. This is a good beginning for a young man and yet, mark you, there are many who have been trained in the ways of godliness who have not continued to walk in them. How often does it seem as if children were dead set against the very things which their parents have loved; and although one would almost have expected that they would have gone in the right way, yet, since grace does not run in the blood, we have deplorable proofs of human depravity even in those who can trace a long line of Christian ancestry. However, it was no small advantage to Jotham that he had godly parents; but it would have been no permanent

---

This sermon was taken from *The Metropolitan Tabernacle Pulpit* and was preached on Thursday evening, August 28, 1873.

131

and eternal advantage to him—it would rather have involved him in greater responsibility without corresponding benefits if it could not also have been said of him that "he prepared his ways before the LORD his God."

And note, next, that *he did not commit the great fault of his father Uzziah.* Uzziah was a good man—an excellent man in many respects; but, in his latter days, he conceived the idea that he would be a priest as well as a king, and he therefore thrust himself into the place that was meant for the priests only. The priests, in great alarm, hastened into the temple of the Lord, where he had gone to burn incense upon the altar of incense, and vehemently protested against his intrusion into their holy office. He was very angry with them; but, suddenly, the deadly leprosy was white upon his brow, for God had smitten him for his daring intrusion. The priests thrust him out of the temple that he might no longer pollute the sanctuary of the Lord; "yea," we read, "himself hasted also to go out, because the Lord had smitten him." Now, if a father—and, specially, a professedly godly father—has committed a great fault, it may be a temptation to his son to fall into the same evil; but, in the case of Jotham, it was not so. He regarded his father's sin rather as a beacon to warn him away from that rock on which Uzziah's life had been wrecked. So, when he was put upon the throne as regent for his father and Uzziah had to be shut up in a house apart as a leper who could not be allowed to mingle with his family and his subjects, Jotham took that as a daily lesson to himself, and he walked the more carefully and humbly before God, preparing his ways, as his father Uzziah had not done on that unfortunate, unhappy day when he went into the temple to offer incense.

It is a great mercy for us when we have seen others sin, if we use their shipwrecks as beacons for ourselves. What fascination should there be in sin? When one bird sees another fall into a snare, we wonder that it should itself be so foolish as to fall into the snare that it can see. Yet have we known men who have seen the sins of their parents, and the sorrow consequent thereon, who have fallen into the same sins themselves. Dear Christian young people, if God has called you by His grace and you have had professing Christian friends whose imperfections you could not help seeing, and seeing with sorrow also the evil effects of their wrong-doing, do not run into the same courses yourselves. Let the painful circumstances which have happened in your own family lead you the more carefully, like Jotham, to prepare your ways before the Lord your God.

Jotham also was *quite a young man when he came into a position of power.* For some years he occupied the place of his father, nominally holding the position of regent, yet really acting as the actual monarch;

and now, at the age of twenty-five, we find him sitting upon the throne of Judah. How needful it is, in young people especially, that the heart and the ways should be prepared before the Lord their God! Yet I retract the expression that it is especially needful for young people to do this, for I have lived long enough to observe that the greatest faults that are ever committed by professedly Christian men are not committed by young people. Most painful is it to me to remember that the worst cases of backsliding and apostasy that I have ever seen in this church have been by old men and middle-aged men—not by young people. For, somehow or other, the young people, if they are truly taught of God, know their weakness, and so they cry to God for help. But it often happens that more experienced people begin to think that they are not likely to fall into the faults and follies of the young; and I care not how old a man may be—even if seven centuries had passed over his head— if he began to trust in himself, he would be a fool, and soon he would have a grievous fall. Yes, even if he had lived as long as Methuselah and all that while had been advancing in the divine life so that he could even fancy that he had reached perfection, the moment he thought so he would be in immanent danger; and the instant he began to think that he should never fall, he would be the very one, above all other men, who would be likely to fall into sin.

They are the strongest who are the weakest in themselves. They are the richest who know how poor they are apart from God. They have the most grace who know how utterly empty they would be of grace if the Lord should ever stay His hand from giving it to them. Growing Christians think nothing of themselves, but full-grown Christians know themselves to be less than nothing. Notwithstanding that there are peculiar dangers associated with youth, and especially with youth placed in a prominent position, here was an instance of a young man and a king, and yet for all that a saint of the right kind, one who "prepared his ways before the Lord his God."

It must be a hard matter to be a king and to be a saint at the same time. The combination has very seldom occurred; and when it has, it has been a prodigious triumph of grace. So, young man, if God shall put you into a place of great responsibility, where you will need much grace to keep you from falling, ask Him for the needful grace, and He will give it to you. Do not ask for an eminent position; let your prayer rather be, "Lead me not into temptation." An eminent position always has a measure of temptation connected with it, so you are justified in praying to be preserved from it. Still, if the position be one which it is your duty to take, take it, and trust to God's grace to keep you there in safety. You are just as safe if God has put you on the cross of St. Paul's as you would be on the pavement below—quite as secure on the top of a mast as you would be in the cabin of the vessel, if God, in His providence, has called you to occupy that position. Only, since there is, in itself, a great danger in the lofty pinnacle, you have the more reason to ask for the needful grace that you may carefully prepare your ways before the Lord, so that you may not bring the greater dishonor upon His name because of the prominence of the position you are called to occupy. King Jotham was a young man and a great man; yet, for all that, he was a saintly man.

Remember also that *he lived in very evil times*. The second verse of this chapter tells us that his own people, whom he had to govern, "did yet corruptly." The parallel passage in 2 Kings 15:35 says that they "sacrificed and burnt incense still in the high places." Their king's good example was not sufficient to reclaim them from the iniquities in which they had so long indulged. It was a great thing for the nation to have a king who worshiped Jehovah, but it was a sad thing that the people still continued to practice their idolatrous rites in the high places, which they were forbidden to do. It is not an easy thing for a man—even a king—to live above his surroundings, and all men are more or less the creatures of circumstances. They are influenced for good or evil by the people round about them; and the most of them fashion their consciences according to the consciences of other people with whom they come in contact.* Even down to a few years ago, there were undoubtedly good men in America who did not think it wrong to buy and sell and hold slaves; the general conscience of the people around them was only up to that level, and their own conscience was not sufficiently enlightened to lift them above their surroundings. They did not see that no man has a right to the labors of another man without adequate payment and that every man has a right to his own liberty. Their conscience had not more light than there was in those who lived round about them. When a man lives in a feverish district, he must have a good sound constitution and be in vigorous health, if he is not to feel some of the evil influence by which he is surrounded; for, if he does not actually take the fever, there is a feverishness, a lethargy, and a condition of *malaise* about him, which he would not have felt if he had been in a more healthful and bracing atmosphere. Yet Jotham appears to have been, through divine grace, a man full of spiritual health, although he lived in a land that was spiritually fever-stricken. He dwelt in the midst of people who were corrupt and yet was himself uncorrupted "because he prepared his ways before the LORD his God."

Some of you, young people, do not know much about this experience because you live, as it were, in a hothouse with Christian parents and with the means of grace all around you. You are like plants in a conservatory; you ought to grow fast. But there are others here who know what the chilly atmosphere of the world means and who know only too well that, after they have been communing with God a little while within these walls, they will have to go where they will hear the voice of blasphemy and profanity and see a thousand things which grieve their spirits day by day and hour by hour. If that is the case with you, my friends, you ought, above all others, to prepare your ways before the Lord your God. I charge you, my brethren, if your occupation takes you among ungodly men—and there are some lawful occupations that will call us where we shall certainly meet with little or nothing that will help us, but much that will hinder us—you must be careful, above all men, to keep a diligent watch upon yourselves and to prepare your ways before the Lord Your God. Your Lord does not pray the Father to take you out of the world, but He does pray that He will keep you from the evil that is in the world. In accordance with His prayer, it ought to be the great aim of your life that you may so live as not to be dragged down to the low level of ungodly men—aye, and not even down to the level of common Christianity. For the level of ordinary Christianity, at this day, far too closely resembles that of the church in Laodicea, which was so nauseous to the Lord. May you, beloved, be a people separated to God, to walk in holiness before Him, and to adorn the doctrine of God your Savior in all things! But if it is to be so with those of you who are placed in circumstances similar to those of Jotham, king of Judah, you must do as he did, you must prepare your ways before the Lord your God.

Once more, as Jotham's surroundings at home were bad, so they were a little further afield, for the adjoining kingdom of Israel was utterly polluted with idolatry and all manner of evil. Jotham was obliged, more or less, to feel the influence of that ungodly neighboring nation. Wherever he looked, he saw very few who prepared their ways before God. Every man went his own way and sought his own wealth or pleasure and oppressed the people around him; but Jotham, like—

> the seraph Abdiel, faithful found
> Among the faithless, faithful only he—

"prepared his ways before the Lord his God." Oh, that such grace as that might be found in abundance in all Christians now, that they might seek to walk in the right road in God's name—not running with the multitude to do evil, but choosing the strait and narrow way which leads to life eternal—with strong resolve determining, the Holy Spirit dwelling in them, that, let others do as they will, as for them and their house, they will serve the Lord, and their ways shall be prepared before Him.

While there were so many unfavorable circumstances that might have been a hindrance to Jotham, there was one fact that must have been very helpful to him. *There were some notable prophets living in Judah in his day.* Isaiah, Hosea, and Micah must all have been well known to Jotham. Isaiah wrote the biography of his father Uzziah, for it is said, in the chapter before that from which our text is taken, "Now the rest of the acts of Uzziah, first and last, did Isaiah the prophet, the son of Amos, write." Jotham therefore knew Isaiah, and I should not wonder if it was one of the greatest helps to the growth of his spiritual life to be able to talk with such a man so full of light and love, with such a clear foresight of the coming of Christ, and such far-reaching visions of the glory of the blessed Gospel day. I should not wonder if Jotham often got away from the people, and got away from the court, and talked alone with this holy man of God. If he did, it was the natural means which God generally uses for the strengthening of His people.

You will be wise, you young Christian professors, if you cultivate Christian companionship. Try to live with those who live with God and sit at the feet of those who sit at the feet of Christ. God may speak through them to your soul; so give heed to what they say, it may be that in giving heed to them, you will be listening to the voice of God Himself. If God does not lack a messenger to deliver His message, let not the messenger lack a hearer to receive the message. Rest assured that you will be most likely to grow in grace when you are earnestly and zealously attending upon the ministry of the Word. The messages of the Lord's chosen prophets probably greatly strengthened the good resolutions and the deep-seated principles of Jotham, and so helped him to prepare his ways before the Lord his God.

This must suffice concerning Jotham's circumstances; they are certainly instructive and suggestive to us.

The Peculiar Distinction of Jotham's Character

It is said that "he prepared his ways before the LORD his God." What does that sentence mean?

Certainly it means, first, that *he resolved to do what God bade him.* He made God's law, God's will, to be the rule that was to govern his life. He desired that what he did should be right in the spirit of the Lord. He did not trouble about being thought to be right by neighboring kings, nor was it his chief care to be thought to be right by the people over whom he ruled. He was not ambitious to be regarded as right by the heathen nations that were near him, but he did want to be right in the sight of God. He had selected, as the rule by which he was to regulate his conduct, God's standard of right and equity and truth and righteousness. Jotham recognized Jehovah as being his God, and he understood that he was bound to obey God—that the first object of his

life ought to be to please Him who first gave him life and who had continued to sustain him in life. It is a grand thing when a man comes to
this decision—that the rule of his life shall be the will of God—that,
from that day forward, God the Holy Spirit working in him, to will and
to do according to God's good pleasure, he will judge that to be right
which God commands and that to be wrong which God forbids, and
that all other rules shall only be rules to him in proportion as they keep
in a line with this rule. Whatever else may be the guide of others,
though it may be a matter of custom or prescription or law or example
of the highest kind, he will not yield to it.

The worst of it is that there are so many who have a number of petty
masters whom they try to serve. One says, "I would not do anything
that is not customary to people in my position." Another says (and this
is a great thing with the most of men), "I should not like to be regarded
as singular or unfashionable." Another asks, "What would society
say?"—that wonderful tyrant of these latter days. Yet another says,
"But my father always did as I am doing," thus putting his father in the
place that ought to be occupied by his God. Another says, "But, you
know, my practice is in accordance with the Council of such-and-such a
Church"; or, "it is in accordance with the decisions of such-and-such a
Synod"; as if councils or synods or anything else had any right to rule
over us, except in so far as their regulations are in harmony with the
will of the Lord our God. It is grand to feel that you are free from all
these fetters and that you can say, "O Lord, I am Your servant; You
have loosed my bonds, and no earthly or hellish power can now make
my spirit bow down before it. Your will commands me, but no other
will does. My knee bows before Your omnipotent majesty. With awe
and reverence I worship You and desire to be subservient in all things
to Your great behests, O Jehovah; but as for these Your creatures, what
are they that I should fear them? Who are they—like the moths that
swiftly pass away and the worms that soon perish—that I should tremble at their frown or court their smile?" God, and God alone, should be
the Christian's master. The rule of his conduct should be the will of the
Lord alone as revealed in the teaching of this blessed Book. Happy will
Christians be and strong in the Lord will they become when they get as
far as that.

But that is not all; that is only the beginning. Jotham had set up the true
standard; he desired to do what was right in the sight of the Lord. But the
next thing was that *he realized God's presence and so acted like a man
who was living consciously in God's presence.* According to the text, he
"prepared his ways before the LORD his God." Beloved, do you and I always realize God's presence in this way? Suppose that, at this very moment, it flashed upon your mind that God was looking into your heart,

could you say that you are loving and thinking of such things as you would be glad to be loving and thinking of, while you were conscious that God was looking upon you? Where have you been today? It is not my place to answer the question for you. Where have you been today? Have you been in such places that you would be glad for God to see you there? Have you been in such a frame of mind that you would be glad for God to see you in that frame of mind? Have you spoken to others in just that spirit and tone that you would like God to hear? He did hear it, remember. He was there; but would you have done as you have done had you been fully conscious, as you ought to have been, that God was there? You know that you sometimes do things that you would not like others to see you doing; and you are startled when somebody finds you so acting. But should it be so? Should it be so? Of course, I do not mean that any of the ordinary work that any of us are doing is of that character; the work that we are doing about the house or in our business should not be a cause of shame to us. I suddenly came upon one of our friends the other day just as she was whitening the front steps. "Oh, dear!" she said, "Mr. Spurgeon, I am sorry you caught me doing this." "My good woman," I said, "I hope that when the Lord comes He will find me at work about my proper duties, just as I have found you. Never mind about your hands; they are as good to shake as ever they were. Let us go into the house and have a little talk together." There is nothing to be ashamed of or to blush at in such work as that; but I should be ashamed and expect others to blush if I found them cheating or doing wrong in some other way or idling their time away as some do. Ought we not to live as though we were expecting the Lord Jesus Christ to come any minute, or as if we knew, as we do know, that God sees us and knows all about us every moment?

But that is not all that we gather concerning Jotham's character. He had accepted the right standard, and he had set that standard in the right light; but now he went further still, for *he was thoughtfully and carefully considerate*. I think that is the gist of the meaning of the expression, "He prepared his ways before the LORD his God." That is to say, he did not go and live in what I may call a careless, happy-go-lucky, hit-or-miss, neck-or-nothing, over-head-and-heels kind of way of living, as some people do. They rush with desperate haste into the battle of life and never seem to give time for thought as to due preparation for the great combat. When any good impulse is upon them, away they go in the right direction at such a speed that you would think they were very eminent and zealous saints; but perhaps tomorrow there will be an evil impulse upon them, and they will go just as fast in the wrong direction. They are so easily influenced by outside circumstances that they are turned either way by those who have power over them, and they are as thoughtless for good as they are for evil. They are heedless and reckless—fine enthusiastic people in their way, but they lack solidity; they are without permanent principles. Like Reuben, being unstable as water, they shall not excel. If a tailor is about to make a suit of clothes, he looks carefully at the cloth before he begins to cut it. But there are some people who seem to use the scissors without any thought at all; they cut out their life-garment at a peradventure. When a man goes into a certain trade, if he hopes to do business, he lays out his plans with considerable forethought and considers his projects with all proper care. If he is to be a successful man of business, he must exercise forethought; and, in the Christian life, we also need much forethought. There ought to be a mapping out of the day, a mapping out of the year, in fact, a mapping out of life itself, and a serious thinking over every part of it. We should often do much better if we did nothing at all. We should frequently make most progress if we stood quite still. Our common proverb is quite correct, "The more haste, the worse speed." It would be a wise plan for each one of us to pause awhile, to put the hand to the brow, and then to say, "Lord, let me hear a voice behind me saying, 'This is the way; walk thou in it.'"

We need to be led where the path seems most plain. Did not the children of Israel make a great mistake in the case of the Gibeanites because it seemed very clear that they must have come from a far country! We generally make our worst mistakes in matters which appear to us to be so plain that we think we do not need direction from God concerning them. If we waited upon God in what we regarded as plain and simple matters, if we made that our rule with regard to them, we should be more likely to go right in the more difficult matters. It would be something like the old proverb, "Take care of the pence, and the pounds will take care of themselves." I mean that if we always took our simplicities to God, we should be quite sure to take our difficulties to Him. I suppose Jotham used, when he was considering a certain course of action, to consider whether he could glorify God by that course of action; and if he thought he could not, he would not take it. When there was proposed to him any mode of doing a certain thing which had to be done, he looked carefully to see whether it was God's mode; and if it was not, he would not adopt that method of doing even the right thing, but would do the right thing in the right way.

But I think there is even more meaning than this in our text. In order to accomplish this preparation of his ways before the Lord his God, *Jotham must have been a man of prayer.* He could not have prepared his ways thus anywhere except at the mercy seat. He must have been in the habit of taking his daily troubles to his God and of seeking guidance from Him in his daily difficulties and of blessing Him for his daily mercies. He must have been in constant communion with his God, or else he could not have ordered his ways aright before Him.

And I should also gather, from our text, that *Jotham was a very fearless, calm, collected, quiet-spirited man*, who was not easily moved, for I find that the marginal reading is, "He established his ways before the LORD his God." He was not fickle-minded, carried about by every wind that blew; but having prepared his heart to serve the Lord, God was pleased to give him a fixity of heart so that he was established in the right way. He could say with David, "My heart is fixed, O God, my heart is fixed"; and the marginal reading there is "prepared." "My heart is prepared, O God." Jotham was steadfast in the right way. What a grand thing it is in our daily life not to be so worried that we are almost driven to distraction and caused to do foolish things through unwise haste. What a mercy it is to be kept calm and quiet in our daily walk before the Lord our God! O dear friends, seek to be thus established before the Lord that, whatever happens to you, your heart shall be so fixed that you shall not be afraid of evil tidings! You can never have power to move the world unless you have a fixed fulcrum for your lever. If your heart is fixed on God, you will be able to move the world, but the world will not be able to move you.

The real reason why Jotham's heart was prepared and established before God was because *his heart was right with God*. And how did his heart get to be right with God? Why, in the same way as yours and mine must—by being created anew. The heart of man, by nature, whether it is Jotham's heart or anybody else's, is a heart of stone. God's almighty grace must make it a heart of flesh, or else a heart of stone it always will remain. If there is anything good in any man, it must have been placed there by a supernatural work of God the Holy Spirit. Job rightly said, "Who can bring a clean thing out of an unclean? not one." Who can bring fixity of heart out of an unstable heart like ours? Who can bring the preparation of our ways before God out of a heart that is, by nature, deceitful above all things and desperately wicked? Jotham earned the commendation in our text because he had been the subject of sovereign grace and continued still to be so. If you and I think that we can prepare our ways before the Lord our God without first resorting to the precious blood of Christ for cleansing and to the Holy Spirit for the renewal of our nature, we shall make a very great mistake. The Lord must first work in us both to will and to do of His good pleasure, and then we must work out our own salvation with fear and trembling; but not until He has thus worked in us can we work it out.

The Peculiar Honor of Jotham's Career

"So Jotham became mighty, because he prepared his ways before the LORD his God." I should imagine, first, that *he was mighty in resolve*. It is a grand thing to have a man of resolves who has a high purpose before him and who means to accomplish it. That is the only man who is worthy to be called a man. As for that poor creature who looks like a man but who has not any mind or will of his own, who has his ear pulled first this way and then that way, whoever likes to pull it—what is the use of such a creature on the face of the earth? But Jotham was not a man of that kind. He sought counsel of the Lord to know what he ought to do; he judged honestly and carefully in the sight of God what was the right thing for him to do, and when he found that out, he put his foot down and said, "That is the thing that I am going to do." It was no use for any of his subjects to say to him, "But perhaps that is not a prudent thing for you to do." He believed that to be right is to be truly prudent. It was no use for any of them to say to Jotham, "But this course of yours may involve us as well as you in serious trouble." He knew perfectly well that, if right sometimes brings trouble, wrong always brings ten times as much; and whenever doing right does bring trouble, it ought to be the delight of the right-hearted to endure that trouble cheerfully. Jotham was strong in resolution as a man has a right to be when he knows that his resolution is a right one. That man, who has prepared his heart and his ways with a single eye to God's glory, resolving only to do the right thing whatever may happen, is the man who has a right to say, "I will," and "I shall." He is the man who, in the long run, will be respected by his fellowmen.

Having ordered his ways before the Lord his God, Jotham had another sort of strength which is a very valuable one—*he was mighty in faith*. He felt this, "I have sincerely desired to glorify God and to walk in His ways, and I am sure that God will carry me through." When he felt that it was right for him to fight the king of the Ammonites, he did fight him in no half-hearted manner, because he felt that if God had bidden him fight, God would surely give him the victory. He went to all his work relying upon God; and oh, how strong is the man who is mighty in faith! You know that you cannot have faith in God about a thing that you know is wrong. If you have ever so slight a suspicion that you are in the wrong, you cannot trust in God concerning it. It is like a little stone in your boot; it may not kill you, but you cannot walk with comfort as long as it is there. And a little question—even a very little one—as to whether you are in the right, cuts the sinews of your strength, and you go limping along, even if you can go at all. If I were speaking to you as a member of a church in which I did not quite believe, if I had to twist my message so as to make it fit the creed that I professed to hold, I should feel wretched. I would not get into such a position as that; I would sooner break stones upon the road any day. But when I feel that I have satisfied the requirements of my conscience in all points and that, if I do err, I do not err willfully or with my eyes open about it, then I can speak with confidence and say, "I know that this is right and that God will help me through with it. It does not at all matter to me what it involves. If it should bring me to poverty or suffering or draw down upon my head misrepresentation and contempt, it does not matter an atom. Wisdom will be justified of all her children. God never did forsake the right yet, and He never will; it must conquer in the long run." If the follower of the right and the true should have to suffer, it shall be a joy to him, for he will thus be all the more a follower of his Lord and Master and of all the true servants of his God who have gone before.

As Jotham was a mighty man in resolution and in faith, he also became *mighty in prayer*. You know that you cannot pray to God with power about a thing that you are not certain is right. It is no use for me to ask the Lord to help me in a matter in which there is something that will grieve His Holy Spirit; it must be a case that I can confidently bring before God if I am to secure His help in it. I am sure that in some trades people could not show the Lord their books; and if they cannot do so and they are getting into difficulties, who can help them out of them? But when all is straight and honest, and the loss, whatever it may be, is caused by no fault of theirs, or when the accusation that is brought against them is nothing but slander, then they can present their petition to God with a clear conscience, and they may rest assured that He will hear them and grant their requests. A man becomes mighty in prayer, as well as in resolution and in faith, whose ways are prepared before the Lord his God.

And such a man also becomes *mighty in action*. He has not that guilty conscience which is the very essence of cowardice. He has gone before God as a sinner and confessed his guilt. He has been washed in the precious blood of Jesus and cleansed from every stain. His heart has been renewed by the Holy Spirit. Although he is not yet perfect, he is perfect in his intention to do the Lord's will; and feeling that he is right and that what he is doing is at God's bidding, he is a terrible man to oppose. He is such a man that no other shall be able to stand against him all the days of his life. He is of that seed royal that Haman will in vain seek to slay, for Haman will be hanged upon the gallows, but Mordecai will be in power in the palace. If a man has thus prepared his ways before the Lord his God, he will be mighty in all that he does, and God will be with him.

And this, dear friends, will make him *mighty against his foes*, as Jotham was against the Ammonites. Oftentimes, they will not even dare to attack him; for "when a man's ways please the Lord, he maketh even his enemies to be at peace with him." They will watch him and go round about him, as Satan went round about Job, but they will find scarcely anything that they can truthfully say against him. Or if they do oppose him, it will be of no use, for he will live them down, if he does not overcome them in any other way. If they bark at him, he will let them bark, for he knows it is the nature of dogs to do so. He will go on his way all the same, as the moon does when the dogs bark at her at night. She never pauses in her course, but goes shining on her way still.

If a man's ways are prepared before the Lord his God, he will be mighty not only against his foes, but he will also be *mighty in the midst of his own people*. Even though Jotham's subjects would not follow him in all respects, they respected him and loved him and made great lamentation over him when he died. Let me say to you young men, if you want to have influence over your fellows, do not take to flattering them and never try to show them how great your talents are or to make them believe you are somebody of importance. We have seen plenty of flashes in the pan, but the darkness has been just as great afterward. Believe me, there is no building up of character except upon sound principles, and there is no building up of influence except upon good character. You must seek, God helping you by His Spirit, to prepare and establish your ways before Him, and then such influence as you ought to have will come to you. When a man tells me that he is very good, I do not believe it. There are certain people, nowadays, who are writing and printing and talking in order to convince us that they are wonderfully holy. I used to think that some of them were so until they said it themselves; but ever since they have said it, I have gravely questioned whether it is true. If anyone whom I met always told me that he was rich—well, if I had dealings with him in business, I should want him to pay cash for everything. When a person tells me that he is holy—well, I trust him as far as I can see him and not much further, for really holy men seldom say anything about their own holiness. They have no need to do so, for it always shows itself. Gold glitters quite enough of itself to show what it is, so there is no need for us to say, "That is gold." You do not need to say of these lamps, "They are bright." They say that for themselves by saying nothing, and simply shining.

I have been preaching to you about a very wonderful example of a gracious man; I wonder whether all here wish to be like him. I am afraid there are some of you who never try to prepare your ways at all; and as for preparing your ways before the Lord, that idea has never struck you yet. And yet, my dear hearer, what can be so safe a way of living as to live in the love of God? And what can be more unhappy than for a man to be out of gear with the omnipotent Creator—to feel, every day you live, that you are forgetting God and are ungrateful to Him and that He is angry with you? I hope that this thought will strike some of you to the heart and make you miserable until all that is altered. The way for it to be altered is for you to submit yourself to God by repentance and by looking to Jesus Christ by faith. May His Holy Spirit lead you to do so now, and then you will begin to live the happiest of lives, for you will be preparing your ways before the Lord your God.

May God bless you all, for Jesus' sake! Amen.

11

Job: The Fair
Portrait of a Saint

My foot hath held his steps, his way have I kept, and not declined.
Neither have I gone back from the commandment of his lips; I have
esteemed the words of his mouth more than my necessary food
(Job 23:11–12).

hus Job speaks of himself, not by way of vaunting, but by way
of vindication. Eliphaz the Temanite and his two companions
had brought distinct charges against Job's character. Because
they saw him in such utter misery, they concluded that his adversity
must have been sent as a punishment for his sin, and therefore they
judged him to be a hypocrite who, under cover of religion, had exer-
cised oppression and tyranny. Zophar had hinted that wickedness was
sweet in Job's mouth and that he hid iniquity under his tongue. Eliphas
charged him with hardness of heart to the poor and dared to say, "Thou
hast taken a pledge from thy brother for nought, and stripped the
naked of their clothing." This last from its very impossibility was
meant to show the extreme meanness to which he falsely imagined that
Job must have descended—how could he strip the naked? He was
evidently firing at random. As neither he nor his companions could
discover any palpable blot in Job upon which they could distinctly lay
their finger, they bespattered him right and left with their groundless
accusations. They made up in venom for the want of evidence to back
their charges. They felt sure that there must be some great sin in him to
have procured such extraordinary afflictions, and therefore by smiting
him all over, they hoped to touch the sore place. Let them stand as a
warning to us never to judge men by their circumstances and never to

---

This sermon was taken from *The Metropolitan Tabernacle Pulpit* and was
preached on Sunday morning, March 7, 1880.

conclude that a man must be wicked because he has fallen from riches to poverty.

Job, however, knew his innocence, and he was determined not to give way to them. He said, "Ye are forgers of lies, physicians of no value. O that ye would altogether hold your peace! and it should be your wisdom." He fought the battle right manfully; not, perhaps, without a little display of temper and self-righteousness, but still with much less of either than any of us would have shown had we been in the same plight, and had we been equally conscious of perfect integrity. He has in this part of his self-defense sketched a fine picture of a man perfect and upright before God. He has set before us the image to which we should seek to be conformed. Here is the high ideal after which every Christian man should strive, and happy shall he be who shall attain to it. Blessed is he who in the hour of his distress, if he be falsely accused, will be able to say with as much truth as the patriarch could, "My foot hath held his steps, his way have I kept, and not declined. Neither have I gone back from the commandment of his lips; I have esteemed the words of his mouth more than my necessary food."

I ask you, first, to inspect the picture of *Job's holy life*, that you may make it your model. After we have done this, we will look a little below the surface, asking the question, "How was he enabled to lead such an admirable life as this? Upon what meat did this great patriarch feed that he had grown so eminent?" We shall find the answer in our second head, *Job's holy sustenance*—"I have esteemed the words of his mouth more than my necessary food." May He, who wrought in Job His patience and integrity, by this our meditation teach us the like virtues by the power of the Holy Spirit.

Job's Holy Life

Note, first, that *Job had been all along a man fearing God and walking after the divine rule*. In the words before us he dwells much upon the things of God—"his steps," "his way," "the commandment of his lips," "the words of his mouth." He was preeminently one that "feared God and eschewed evil." He knew God to be the Lord and worthy to be served, and therefore he lived in obedience to His law, which was written upon his instructed conscience. His way was God's way; he chose that course which the Lord commanded. He did not seek his own pleasure nor the carrying out of his own will. Neither did he follow the fashion of the times, nor conform himself to the ruling opinion or custom of the age in which he lived. Fashion and custom were nothing to him; he knew no rule but the will of the Almighty. Like some tall cliff which breasts the flood, he stood out almost alone, a witness for God in an idolatrous world. He owned the living God and lived "as seeing him who is invisible."

God's will had taken the helm of the vessel, and the ship was steered in God's course according to the divine compass of infallible justice and the unerring chart of the divine will. This is a great point to begin with; it is, indeed, the only sure basis of a noble character.

Ask the man who seeks to be the architect of a great and honorable character this question—Where do you place God? Is He second with you? Ah, then, in the judgment of those whose view comprehends all human relationships, you will lead a very secondary kind of life, for the first and most urgent obligation of your being will be disregarded. But is God first with you? Is this your determination, "As for me and my house, we will serve the Lord"? Do you seek first the kingdom of God and His righteousness? If so, you are laying the foundation for a whole or holy character, for you begin by acknowledging your highest responsibility. In this respect you will find that "the fear of the Lord is the beginning of wisdom." Whether the way be rough or smooth, uphill or down dale, through green pastures or burning deserts, let God's way be your way. Where the fiery cloudy pillar of His providence leads, be sure to follow, and where His holy statutes command, there promptly go. Ask the Lord to let you hear His Spirit speak like a voice behind you saying, "This is the way, walk ye in it." As soon as you see from the Scriptures or from conscience or from providence what the will of the Lord is, make haste and delay not to keep His commandments. Set the Lord always before you. Have respect to His statutes at all times, and in all your ways acknowledge Him. No man will be able to look back upon his life with complacency unless God has been sitting upon the throne of his heart and ruling all his thoughts, aims, and actions. Unless he can say with David, "My soul hath kept thy testimonies and I love them exceedingly," he will find much to weep over and little with which to answer his accusers.

We must follow the Lord's way, or our end will be destruction. We must take hold upon Christ's steps, or our feet will soon be in slippery places. We must reverence God's words, or our own words will be idle and full of vanity. We must keep God's commands, or we shall be destitute of that holiness without which no man shall see the Lord. I set not forth obedience to the law as the way of salvation, but I speak to those who profess to be saved already by faith in Christ Jesus. I remind all of you who are numbered with the company of believes that if you are Christ's disciples, you will bring forth the fruits of holiness, and if you are God's children, you will be like your Father. Godliness breeds Godlikeness. The fear of God leads to imitation of God, and where this is not so, the root of the matter is lacking. The scriptural rule is "by their fruits ye shall know them," and by this we must examine ourselves.

Let us now consider Job's first sentence. He says, "*My foot hath held his steps.*" This expression sets forth great carefulness. He had watched every step of God, that is to say, he had been minute as to particulars, observing each precept, which he looked upon as being a footprint which the Lord had made for him to set his foot in and observing, also, each detail of the great example of his God. For in so far as God is imitable, He is the great example of His people, as He says— "Be ye holy, for I am holy"; and again, "Be ye perfect, even as your Father which is in heaven is perfect." Job had observed the steps of God's justice that he might be just; the steps of God's mercy that he might be pitiful and compassionate; the steps of God's bounty that he might never be guilty of churlishness or want of liberality; and the steps of God's truth that he might never deceive. He had watched God's steps of forgiveness that he might forgive his adversaries and God's steps of benevolence that he might also do good and communicate, according to his ability, to all that were in need. In consequence of this he became eyes to the blind and feet to the lame; he delivered the poor that cried and the fatherless and him that had none to help. The blessing of him that was ready to perish came upon him, and he caused the widow's heart to sing for joy.

"My foot," he says, "hath held his steps." He means that he had labored to be exact in his obedience toward God and in his imitation of the divine character. Beloved, we shall do well if we are to the minutest point hourly observant of the precepts and example of God in all things. We must follow not only the right road but His footprints in that road. We are to be obedient to our heavenly Father not only in some things but in all things—not in some place but in all places, abroad and at home, in business and in devotion, in the words of our lips and in the thoughts of our hearts. There is no holy walking without careful watching. Depend upon it, no man was ever good by chance, nor did anyone ever become like the Lord Jesus by a happy accident. "I put gold into the furnace," said Aaron, "and there came out this calf," but nobody believed him. If the image was like a calf, it was because he had shaped it with a graving tool. If it is not to be believed that metal will of itself take the form of a calf, much less will character assume the likeness of God Himself, as we see it in the Lord Jesus. The pattern is too rich and rare, too elaborate and perfect, ever to be reproduced by a careless, half-awakened trifler. No, we must give all our heart and mind and soul and strength to this business and watch every step, or else our walk will not be close with God nor pleasing in His sight. O to be able to say, "My foot hath held his steps."

Notice here that the expression has something in it of tenacity, he speaks of taking hold upon God's steps. The idea needs to be lit up by the illustration contained in the original expression. You must go to mountainous regions to understand it. In very rough ways a person may walk all the better for having no shoes to his feet. I sometimes pitied the women of Mentone coming down the rough places of the mountains barefooted, carrying heavy loads upon their heads, but I ceased to pity them when I observed that most of them had a capital pair of shoes in the basket at the top. I perceived as I watched them that they could stand where I slipped, because their feet took hold upon the rock, almost like another pair of hands. Barefooted they could safely stand and readily climb where feet encased after our fashion would never carry them. Many Orientals have a power of grasp in their feet which we appear to have lost from want of use. An Arab in taking a determined stand actually seems to grasp the ground with his toes. Roberts tells us in his well-known *Illustrations* that Easterns, instead of stooping to pick up things from the ground with their fingers, will take them up with their toes. He tells of a criminal condemned to be beheaded, who, in order to stand firm when about to die, grasped a shrub with his foot. Job declares that he took hold of God's steps and thus secured a firm footing. He had a hearty grip of holiness, even as David said, "I have stuck unto thy testimonies." That eminent scholar Dr. Good renders the passage, "in his steps will I *rivet* my feet." He would set them as fast in the footprints of truth and righteousness as if they were riveted there, so firm was his grip upon that holy way which his heart had chosen.

This is exactly what we need to do with regard to holiness; we must feel about for it with a sensitive conscience to know where it is, and when we know it, we must seize upon it eagerly and hold to it as for our life. The way of holiness is often craggy, and Satan tries to make it very slippery. Unless we can take hold of God's steps, we shall soon slip with our feet and bring grievous injury upon ourselves and dishonor to His holy name. Beloved, to make up a holy character there must be a tenacious adherence to integrity and piety. You must not be one that can be blown off his feet by the hope of a little gain or by the threatening breath of an ungodly man. You must stand fast and stand firm, and against all pressure and blandishment you must seize and grasp the precepts of the Lord and abide in them, riveted to them. Standfast is one of the best soldiers in the Prince Immanuel's army, and one of the most fit to be trusted with the colors of his regiment. "Having done all, still stand."

To make a holy character we must take hold of the steps of God in the sense of promptness and speed. Here again I must take you to the East to get the illustration. They say of a man who closely imitates his religious teacher, "his feet have laid hold of his master's steps," meaning that he so closely follows his teacher that he seems to take hold of his heels. This is a blessed thing indeed, when grace enables us to follow our Lord closely. There is His foot, and close behind it is ours; and there again He takes another step, and we plant our feet where He has planted His. A very beautiful motto is hung up in our infant classroom at the Stocknell Orphanage, *"What would Jesus do?"* Not only may children take it as their guide, but all of us may do the same, whatever our age. "What would Jesus do?" If you desire to know what you ought to do under any circumstances, imagine Jesus to be in that position and then think, "What would Jesus do? For what Jesus would do that ought I to do." In following Jesus we are following God, for in Christ Jesus the brightness of the Father's glory is best seen. Our example is our Lord and Master, Jesus the Son of God, and therefore this question is but a beam from our guiding star. Ask in all cases—"What would Jesus do?" That unties the knot of all moral difficulty in the most practical way, and does it so simply that no great wit or wisdom will be needed. May God's Holy Spirit help us to copy the line which Jesus has written, even as scholars imitate their writing master in each stroke and line and mark and dot.

Oh, when we come to die and have to look back upon our lives, it will be a blessed thing to have followed the Lord fully. They are happy who follow the Lamb whithersoever He goes. Blessed are they in life and death of whom it can be said—as he was so were they also in this world. Though misunderstood and misrepresented, yet they were honest imitators of their Lord. Such a true-hearted Christian can say, "He knows the way that I take. He tried me, and I came forth as gold. My foot has held His steps." Many a sorrow will you avoid if you keep close at your Master's heel. You know what came of Peter's following afar off; try what will come of close walking with Jesus. Abide in Him and let His words abide in you, so shall you be His disciples. You dare not trust in your works and will not think of doing so, yet will you bless God that, being saved by His grace, you were enabled to bring forth the fruits of the Spirit by a close and exact following of the steps of your Lord.

Three things, then, we get in the first sentence—an exactness of obedience, a tenacity of grip upon that which is good, and a promptness in endeavoring to keep touch with God and to follow Him in all respects. May these things be in us and abound.

We now pass on to the second sentence. I am afraid you will say, "Spare us, for even to the first sentence we have not yet attained." Labor after it then, beloved; forgetting the things that are behind except to weep over them, press forward to that which is before. May God give you those sensitive grasping feet which we have tried to describe, feet that take hold on the Lord's way, and may you throughout life keep that hold; for "blessed are the undefiled in the way, who walk in the law of the Lord."

The next sentence runs thus: "*His way have I kept*"; that is to say, Job had adhered to God's way as the rule of his life. When he knew that such-and-such a thing was the mind of God, either by his conscience telling him that it was right or by a divine revelation, then he obeyed the intimation and kept to it. He did not go out of God's way to indulge his own fancies or to follow some supposed leader. To God's way he kept from his youth, even until the time when the Lord Himself said of him, "Hast thou considered my servant Job, a perfect and an upright man, one that feareth God, and escheweth evil?" The Lord gave him this character to the Devil, who could not deny it and did not attempt to do so, but only muttered, "Doth Job serve God for nought? Hast thou not set a hedge about him and all that he hath?" When he uttered our text, Job could have replied to the malicious accuser that, even when God had broken down his hedges and laid him waste, he had not sinned nor charged God foolishly. He heeded not his wife's rash counsels to curse God and die, but he still blessed the divine name even though everything was taken from him. What noble words are those: "Naked came I out of my mother's womb, and naked shall I return thither: the Lord gave, and the Lord hath taken away; blessed be the name of the Lord." Though bereft of all earthly comfort, he did not forsake the way of holiness, but still kept to his God.

Keeping to the way signifies not simply adherence, but continuance and progress in it. Job had gone on in the ways of God year after year. He had not grown tired of holiness nor weary of devotion, neither had he grown sick of what men call straight-laced piety. He had kept the way of God on and on and on, delighting in what Coverdale's version calls God's "high street"—the highway of holiness. The further he went the more pleasure he took in it, and the more easy he found it to his feet, for God was with him and kept him, and so he kept God's way. "Thy way have I kept." He means that notwithstanding there were difficulties in the way he persevered in it. It was stormy weather, but Job kept to the old road; the sleet beat in his face, but he kept His way. He had gone that path in fair weather, and he was not going to forsake his God now that the storms were out; and so he kept His way. Then the scene changed, the sun was warm, and all the air was redolent with perfume and merry with the song of birds, but Job kept His way. If God's providence flooded his sky with sunshine, he did not forsake God because of prosperity, as some do, but kept His way—kept His way when it was rough, kept His way when it was smooth. When he met with adversities, he did not turn into a byroad but traveled the King's highway where a man is safest, for those who dare to assail him will have to answer for it to a higher power. The high street of holiness is safe because the King's guarantee is given that "no lion shall be there, neither shall any ravenous beast go up thereon." The righteous shall hold on His way, and so did Job, come fair, come foul. When there were others in the road with him, and when there were none, he kept His way. He would not even turn aside for those three good men, or men who thought themselves good, who sat by the wayside and miserably comforted, that is to say, tormented him. He kept God's way, as one whose mind is made up and whose face is set like a flint. There was no turning him, he would fight his way if he could not have it peaceably.

I like a man whose mind is set upon being right with God, a self-contained man by God's grace, who does not want patting on the back and encouraging and who, on the other hand, does not care if he is frowned at but has counted the cost and abides by it. Give me a man who has a backbone, a brave fellow who has grit in him. It is well for a professor when God has put some soul into him and made a man of him, for if a Christian man is not a man as well as a Christian, he will not long remain a Christian man. Job was firm, a well-made character that did not shrink in the wetting. He believed his God. He knew God's way, and he kept to it under all circumstances from his first start in life even until that day when he sat on a dunghill and transformed it into a throne, whereon he reigned as among all mere men the peerless prince of patience. You have heard of the patience of Job and of this as one part of it, that he kept the way of the Lord.

Now, dear brethren, on this second clause let me utter this word of self-examination. Have we kept God's way? Have we got into it and do we mean to keep it still? Some are soon hot and soon cold; some set out for the New Jerusalem like Pliable, very eagerly, but the first slough of despond they tumble into shakes their resolution, and they crawl out on the homeward side and go back to the world again. There will be no comfort in such temporary religion, but dreadful misery when we come to consider it on a dying bed. Changeful Pliables will find it hard to die. O to be constant even to the end, so as to say, "My foot hath held his steps, his way have I kept." God grant us grace to do it by his Spirit abiding in us.

The third clause is, "*And not declined*," by which I understand that he had not declined *from* the way of holiness nor declined *in* the way. First, he had not declined from it. He had not turned to the right hand nor to the left. Some turn away from God's way to the right hand by doing more than God's Word has bidden them do—such as invent religious ceremonies and vows and bonds and become superstitious, falling under the bondage of priestcraft and being led into will-worship and things that are not scriptural. This is as truly wandering as going out of the road to the left would be. Ah, dear friends, keep to the simplicity of the Bible. This is an age in which Holy Scripture is very little accounted of. If a church chooses to invent a ceremony, men fall into it and practice it as if it were God's ordinance. Aye, and if neither church nor law recognize the performance, yet if certain self-willed priests choose to burn candles and to wear all sorts of bedizenments and bow and cringe and march in procession, there are plenty of simpletons who will go whichever way their clergyman chooses, even if he should lead them into downright heathenism. "Follow my leader" is the game of the day, but "Follow my God" is the motto of a true Christian. Job had not turned to the right.

Nor had Job turned to the left. He had not been lax in observing God's commandments. He had shunned omission as well as commission. This is a very heart-searching matter; for how many there are whose greatest sins lie in omission. And remember, sins of omission, though they sit very light on many consciences, and though the bulk of professors do not even think them sins, are the very sins for which men will be condemned at the last. How do I prove that? What said the great Judge? "I was an hungered and ye gave me no meat, I was thirsty and ye gave me no drink, sick and in prison and ye visited me not." It was what they did not do that cursed them more than what they did do. So look you well to it, and pray God that you may not decline from the way of His precepts, from Jesus who, Himself, is the one and only way.

Furthermore, I take it Job means that he had not even declined *in* that way. He did not begin with running hard and then get out of breath and sit by the wayside and say, "Rest and be thankful"; but he kept up the pace and did not decline. If he was warm and zealous once, he remained warm and zealous; if he was indefatigable in service, he did not gradually tone down into a sluggard, but he could say, "I have not declined." Whereas we ought to make advances toward heaven, there are many who are, after twenty years profession, no more forward than they were, but perhaps in a worse state. Oh, beware of a decline. We were accustomed to use that term years ago to signify the commencement of a consumption or perhaps the effects of it; and indeed, a decline in the soul often leads on to a deadly consumption. In a spiritual consumption the very life of religion seems to ebb out by little and little. The man does not die by a wound that stabs his reputation but by a secret weakness within him, which eats at the vitals of godliness and leaves the outward surface fair. God save us from declining.

I am sure, dear friends, we cannot many of us afford to decline much, for we are none too earnest, none too much alive now. This is one of the great faults of churches, so many of the members are in a decline that the church becomes a hospital instead of a barracks. Many professors are not what they were at first; they were very promising young men, but they are not performing old men. We are pleased to see the flowers on our fruit trees, but they disappoint us unless they knit into fruit, and we are not satisfied even then unless the fruit ripens to a mellow sweetness. We do not make orchards for the sake of blossoms; we want apples. So is it with the garden of grace, our Lord comes seeking fruit, and instead thereof He often finds nothing but leaves. May God grant to us that we may not decline from the highest standard we have ever reached. "I would," said the Lord of the church of Laodicea, "that thou wert either cold or hot." Oh, you lukewarm ones take that warning to heart. Remember, Jesus cannot endure you; He will spew you out of His mouth; you make Him sick to think of you. If you were downright cold, He would understand you; if you were hot, He would delight in you; but being neither cold nor hot He is sick at the thought of you. He cannot endure you; and indeed, when we think of what the Lord has done for us, it is enough to make us sick to think that anyone should drag on in a cold, inanimate manner in His service, who loved us and gave Himself for us.

Some decline because they become poor. They even stay from worship on that account. I hope none of you say, "I do not like to come to the Tabernacle because I have not fit clothes to come in." As I have often said, any clothes are fit for a man to come here in if he has paid for them. Let each come by all manner of means in such garments as he has, and he shall be welcome. But I do know some very poor professors who, in the extremity of their anxiety and trouble, instead of flying to God, fly from Him. This is very sad. The poorer you are, the more you want the rich consolations of grace. Do not let this temptation overcome you; but if you are as poor as Job, be as resolved as he to keep to the Lord's way and not decline. Others fly from their religion because they grow rich. They say that three generations never will come on wheels to a dissenting place of worship, and it has proved to be sadly true in many instances, though I have no cause to complain of you as yet. Some persons when they rise in the world turn up their noses at their poor friends. If any of you do so, you will be worthy of pity, if not of contempt. If you forsake the ways of God for the fashion of the world, you will be poor gainers by your wealth. The Lord keep you from such a decline. Many decline because they conform to the fashion of the world, and the way of the world is not the way of God. Does not James say, "Know ye not that the friendship of the world is enmity with God? Whosoever therefore will be a friend of the world is the enemy of God." Others wander because they get into ill company, among witty people or clever people or hospitable people, who are not gracious people. Such society is dangerous. People whom we esteem, but whom God does not esteem, are a great snare. It is very perilous to love those who love not God. He shall not be my bosom friend who is not God's friend, for I shall probably do him but little service, and he will do me much harm. May the grace of God prevent your growing cold from any of these causes, and may you be able to say, "I have not declined."

One more sentence remains, *"Neither have I gone back from the commandment of his lips"*; that is to say, as he had not slackened his pace, so much less had he turned back. May none of you ever go back. This is the most cutting grief of a pastor, that certain persons come in among us, and even come to the front, who after awhile turn back and walk no more with us. We know, as John says, "They went out from us, but they were not of us; for if they had been of us, they would no doubt have continued with us; but they went out, that they might be made manifest that they were not all of us." Yet what anguish it causes when we see apostates among us and know their doom. Take heed, brethren, lest there be in any of you an evil heart of unbelief in departing from the living God. Let Lot's wife be a warning. Season your souls with a fragment of salt from that pillar, and it may keep you from corruption.

Remember that you can turn back, not only from all the commandments, and so become an utter apostate, but there is such a thing as backing at single commandments. You know the precept to be right, but you cannot face it; you look at it and look at it and look at it, and then go back, back, back from it, refusing to obey. Job had never done so. If it was God's command, he went forward to perform it. It may be that it seems impossible to go forward in the path of duty, but if you have faith, you are to go on whatever the difficulty may be. Leap over the wall before you, dear friends, even if it seem to be a wall of granite. God will clear the road. By faith the Israelites went through the Red Sea as on dry land. It is ours to do what God bids us, as He bids us, when He bids us, and no hurt can come of it. Strength equal to our day shall be given, only let us cry "Forward!" and push on.

Here just one other word. Let us take heed to ourselves that we do not go back, for going back is dangerous. We have no armor for our back, no promise of protection in retreat. Going back is ignoble and base. To have had a grand idea and then to turn back from it like a whipped cur is disgraceful. Shame on the man who dares not be a Christian. Even sinners and ungodly men point at the man who put his hand to the plow and looked back, and was not worthy of the kingdom. Indeed, it is fatal; for the Lord has said, "If any man draw back, my soul shall have no pleasure in him." Forward! Forward! though death and hell obstruct the way, for backward is defeat, destruction, despair. O God, grant us of Your grace that when we come to the end of life we may say with joy, "I have not gone back from Your commandment." The covenant promises persevering grace, and it shall be yours, only look well that you trifle not with this grace.

There is the picture which Job has sketched. Hang it up on the wall of your memory, and God help you to paint after this old master, whose skill is unrivaled.

Job's Holy Sustenance

"I have esteemed the words of his mouth more than my necessary food."

First, then, *God spoke to Job.* Did God ever speak to you? I do not suppose Job had a single page of inspired writing. Probably he had not even seen the first books of Moses; he may have done so, but probably he had not. God spoke to him. Did He ever speak to you? No man will ever serve God aright unless God has spoken to him. You have the Bible, and God speaks in that Book and through it; but mind you do not rest in the printed letter without discerning its spirit. You must try to hear God's voice in the printed letter. "God hath in these last days spoken unto us by his Son"; but oh, pray that this divine Son may speak by the Holy Spirit right into your heart. Anything which keeps you from personal contact with Jesus robs you of the best blessing. The Romanist says he uses a crucifix to help him to remember Christ, and then his prayers often stop at the crucifix and do not get to Christ. In like manner you can make an idol of your Bible by using the mere words as a substitute for God's voice to you. The Book is to help you to remember God, but if you stick in the mere letter and get not to God at all, you misuse the sacred Word. When the Spirit of God speaks a text right into the soul, when God Himself takes the promise or the precept and sends it with living energy into the heart, this is that which makes a man have a reverence for the Word. He feels its awful majesty, its divine supremacy, and while he trembles at it, he rejoices and goes forward to obey because God has spoken to him. Dear friends, when God speaks, be sure that you have open ears to hear, for oftentimes He speaks and men regard Him not. In a vision of the night when deep sleep falls upon men, God has spoken to His prophets, but now He speaks by His word, applying it to the heart with power by His Spirit. If God speaks but little to us, it is because we are dull of hearing. Renewed hearts are never long without a whisper from the Lord. He is not a dumb God nor is He so far away that we cannot hear Him. They that keep His ways and hold His steps, as Job did, shall hear many of His words to their soul's delight and profit. God's having spoken to Job was the secret of his consistently holy life.

Then note, that *what God had spoken to him he treasured up.* He says in the Hebrew that he had hid God's word more than ever he had hidden his necessary food. They had to hide grain away in those days to guard it from wandering Arabs. Job had been more careful to store up

God's word than to store up his wheat and his barley, more anxious to preserve the memory of what God had spoken than to garner his harvests. Do you treasure up what God has spoken? Do you study the Word? Do you read it? Oh, how little do we search it compared with what we ought to do. Do you meditate on it? Do you suck out its secret sweets? Do you store up its essence as bees gather the life-blood of flowers and hoard up their honey for winter food? Bible study is the metal that makes a Christian; this is the strong meat on which holy men are nourished; this is that which makes the bone and sinew of men who keep God's way in defiance of every adversary. God spoke to Job, and Job treasured up His words.

We learn from our version of the text that *Job lived on God's Word*; he reckoned it to be better to him than his necessary food. He ate it. This is an art which some do not understand—eating the Word of the Lord. Some look at the surface of the Scriptures; some pull the Scriptures to pieces without mercy; some cut the heavenly bread into dice pieces and show their cleverness; some pick it over for plums, like children with a cake; but blessed is he that makes it his meat and drink. He takes the Word of God to be what is, namely, a Word from the mouth of the Eternal, and he says, "God is speaking to me in this, and I will satisfy my soul upon it. I do not want anything better than this, anything truer than this, anything safer than this, but having gotten this, it shall abide in me, in my heart, in the very bowels of my life. It shall be interwoven with the fabric of my being."

But the text adds that he esteemed it more than his *necessary* food. Not more than dainties only, for those are superfluities, but more than his necessary food, and you know that a man's necessary food is a thing which he esteems very highly. He must have it. What, take away my bread? says he, as if this could not be borne. To take the bread out of a poor man's mouth is looked upon as the highest kind of villainy. But Job would sooner that they took the bread out of his mouth than the Word of God out of his heart. He thought more of it than of his needful food, and I suppose it was because meat would only sustain his body, but the Word of God feeds the soul. The nourishment given by bread is soon gone, but the nourishment given by the Word of God abides in us and makes us to live forever. The natural life is more than meat, but our spiritual life feeds on meat even nobler than itself, for it feeds on the bread of heaven, the person of the Lord Jesus. Bread is sweet to the hungry man, but we are not always hungry, and sometimes we have no appetite; but the best of God's Word is that he who lives near to God has always an appetite for it, and the more he eats of it the more he can eat.

I do confess I have often fed upon God's Word when I have had no appetite for it, until I have gained an appetite. I have grown hungry in proportion as I have felt satisfied. My emptiness seemed to kill my hunger, but as I have been revived by the Word, I have longed for more. So it is written, "Blessed are they that hunger and thirst after righteousness, for they shall be filled." When they are filled, they shall continue to enjoy the benediction, for they shall hunger and thirst still though filled with grace. God's Word is sweeter to the taste than bread to a hungry man, and its sweetness never cloys, though it dwells long on the palate. You cannot be always eating bread, but you can always feed on the Word of God. You cannot eat all the meat that is set before you, your capacity is limited that way, and none but a glutton wishes it otherwise. But oh, you may be ravenous of God's Word, and devour it all and yet have no surfeit. You are like a little mouse in a great cheese, and you shall have permission to eat it all, though it be a thousand times greater than yourself. Though God's thoughts are greater than your thoughts and His ways are greater than your ways, yet may His ways be in your heart and your heart in His ways. You may be filled with all the fullness of God, though it seems a paradox. His fullness is greater than you, and all His fullness is infinitely greater than you, yet you may be filled with all the fullness of God. So that the Word of God is better than our necessary food; it has qualities which our necessary food has not.

No more, except it be this: you cannot be holy, my brethren, unless you do in secret live upon the blessed Word of God, and you will not live on it unless it comes to you as the word *of His mouth*. It is very sweet to get a letter from home when you are far away. It is like a bunch of fresh flowers in winter time. A letter from the dear one at home is as music heard over the water; but half-a-dozen words from that dear mouth are better than a score pages of manuscript, for there is a sweetness about the look and the tone which paper cannot carry. Now, I want you to get the Bible to be not a book only but a speaking trumpet, through which God speaks from afar to you, so that you may catch the very tones of His voice. You must read the Word of God to this end, for it is while reading, meditating, and studying, and seeking to dip yourself into its spirit that it seems suddenly to change from a written book into a talking book or phonograph. It whispers to you or thunders at you as though God had hidden Himself among its leaves and spoke to your condition, as though Jesus who feeds among the lilies had made the chapters to be lily beds and had come to feed there. Ask Jesus to cause His Word to come fresh from His own mouth to your soul; and if it be so and you thus live in daily communion with a personal Christ, my brethren, you will then with your feet take hold upon His steps. Then will you keep His way; then will you never decline or go back from His commandments, but you will make good speed in your pilgrim way to the eternal city. May the Holy Spirit daily be with you. May every one of you live under His sacred bedewing, and be fruitful in every good word and work. Amen and amen.